American Corporate Identity

The State of the Art in the 80s

David E. Carter
Editor

Art Direction Book Co.
10 E. 39th Street
New York, N.Y. 10016

ISBN: 0-88108-026-8

LCCC #: 85-072864

Printed in Japan

American Corporate Identity has encountered a number of changes in the last few years.
This book includes selected entries in a competition which was held in 1984 to select the current examples of corporate identity which represent "the state of the art."

Table of Contents

Complete Identity Programs

Client Alia, the Royal Jordanian Airline
Designer Steve Harding
Design Firm 3D/International

Client BankAmerica Corporation
Designer Design Systems Group
Design Firm Landor Associates

Bank of America

Client Citizen's Fidelity Bank
Designer John DiGianni
Design Firm Gianninoto Associates

Client Corvus Systems
Designers Howard York and Dale Brock
Design Firm S&O Consultants

Client Firstar Corporation
Design Firm Lee & Young
Communications, Inc.

Client Fleet Financial Group
Designer Special Projects Group
Design Firm Landor Associates

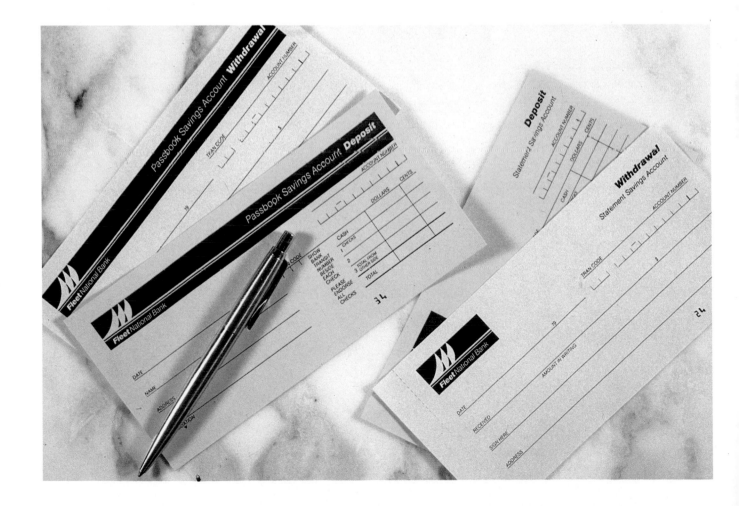

Client GAF Corporation
Designer Paul D. Miller
Design Firm Paul D. Miller Enterprises, Inc.

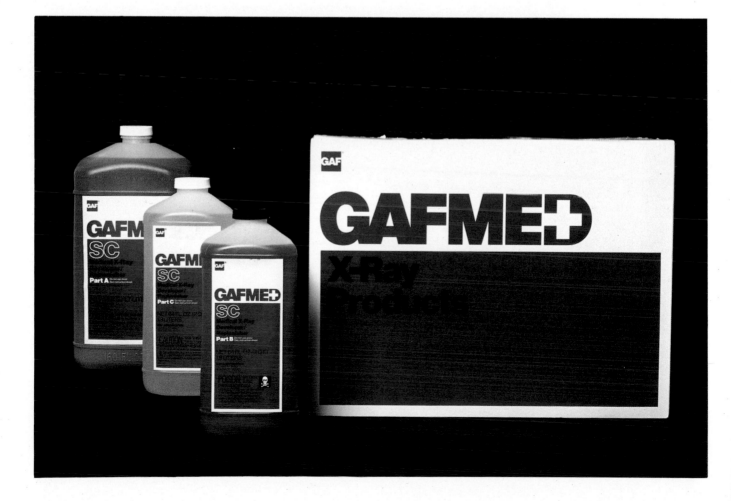

Client Harvest Manor Cafeteria/
Banquet Facility
Designers Frank S. Morris, Jr.
Dr. William A. Jones, Jr.
Design Firm F. Morris Advertising & Design

Client Hawaiian Air
Designer Marketing Design Group
Design Firm Landor Associates

HAWAIIAN AIR

Client Holiday Inn Crowne Plaza
Designers Howard York, Creative Director
          Dale Brock, Project Director
Design Firm S&O Consultants

HOLIDAY INN
CROWNE PLAZA

Client Jockey International
Designers Les Grebetz, Jo Ellen Mason
Design Firm Design Investigation Group

Client Minnesota Zoo
Designers Lance Wyman, Stephen Schlott,
Linda Iskander
Design Firm Lance Wyman Ltd.

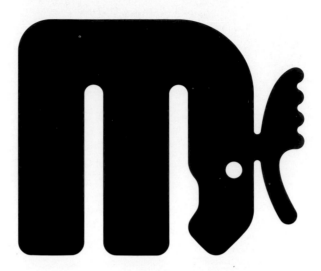

Client National Zoological Park
Designers Lance Wyman, Bill Cannan,
        Brian Flahive, Tucker Viemeister,
        Tom DeMonse
Design Firm Wyman & Cannan Co. Ltd.

Client Norwest Bancorp
Designers Howard York, Creative Director
Fran Koenig, Design Director
Design Firm S&O Consultants

Client Pacific Telephone
Designer Special Projects Group
Design Firm Landor Associates

PACIFIC✻BELL℠

Client Power Packaging Inc.
Designer Les Grebetz
Design Firm Design Investigation Group

Power Packaging Inc.

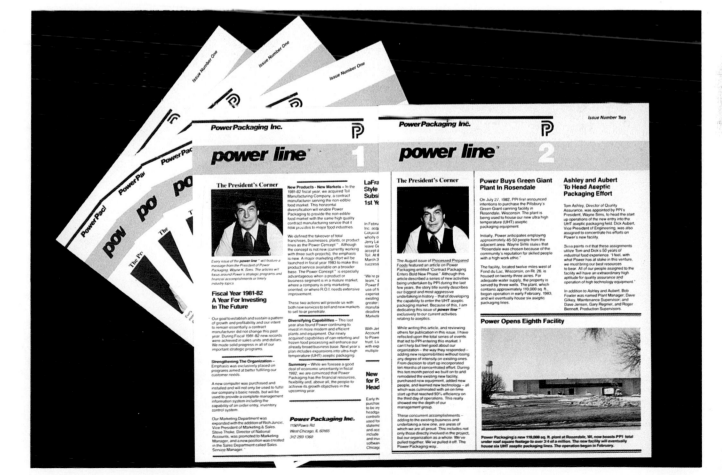

Client The Prudential Insurance Co.
of America
Design Firm Lee & Young
Communications, Inc.

1896   1900's   1920's   1940's

1950's   1970's   1977   1984

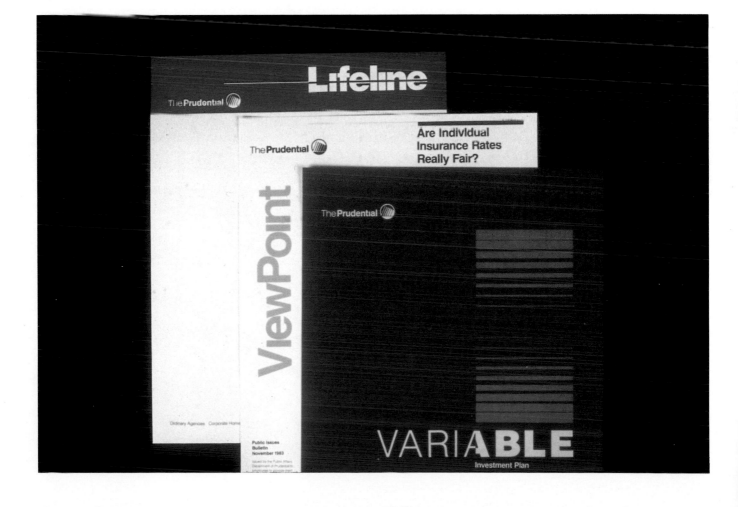

Client Staten Island Zoo
Designer Vincent J. Mielcarek
Design Firm Mielcarek Advertising

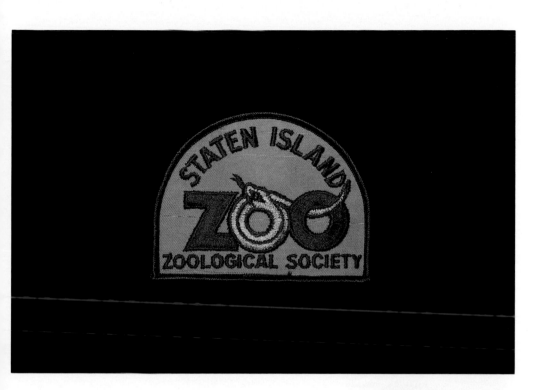

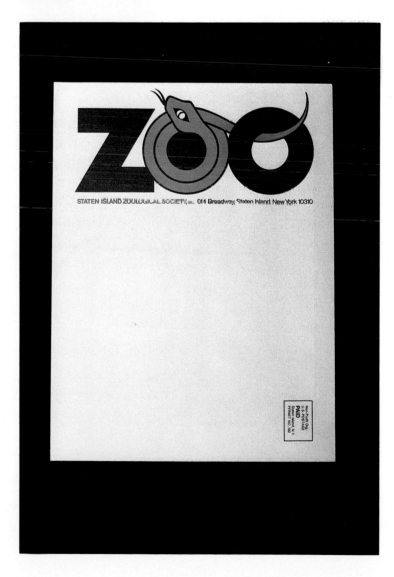

STATEN ISLAND ZOOLOGICAL SOCIETY, INC. 614 Broadway, Staten Island, New York 10310

Client Stevedoring Services of America
Designers John Hornall, Jack Anderson,
                Rey Sabado
Design Firm John Hornall Design Works

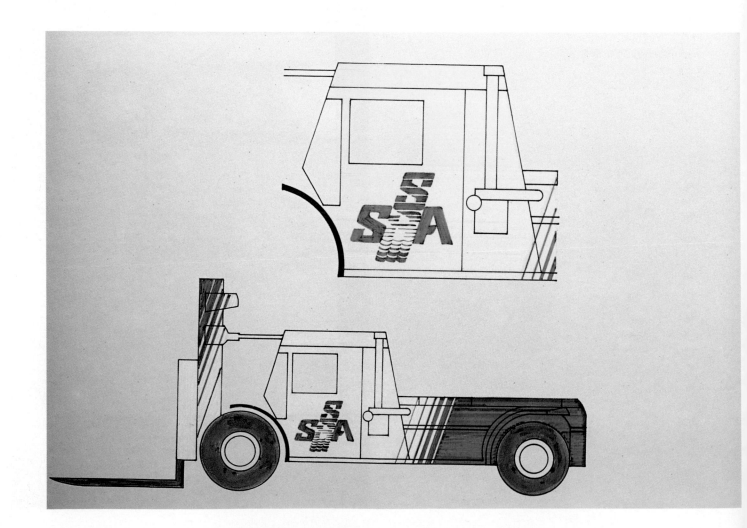

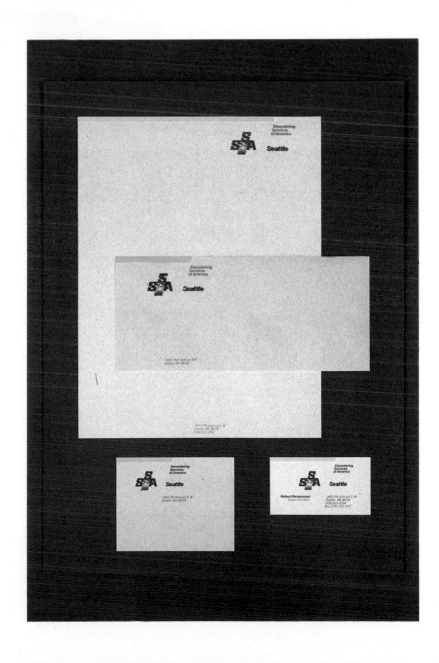

Client The Seven-Up Company
Designer Tobacco/Beverage/Spirits Group
Design Firm Landor Associates

Client Twentieth Century Fox Film Corp.
Designer Special Projects Group
Design Firm Landor Associates

TWENTIETH CENTURY FOX
FILM CORPORATION

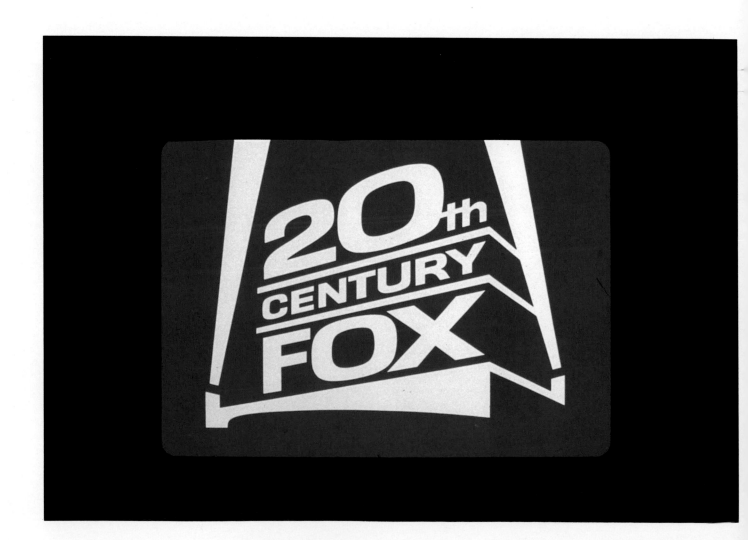

Client Westin Hotels
Designer Special Projects Group
Design Firm Landor Associates

WESTIN HOTELS

Client Westmin Resources Ltd.
Design Firm Lee & Young
Communications, Inc.

Corporate Identity Manuals

Client Agmax
Designers Greg Bauer, Denise Spaulding
Design Firm David E. Carter Corporate
Communications, Inc.

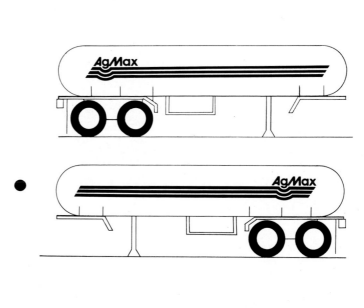

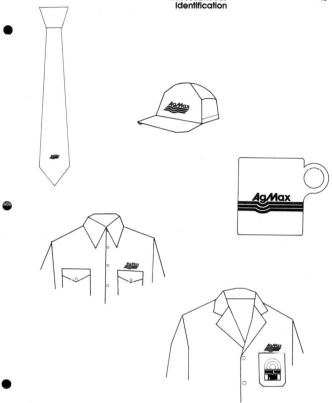

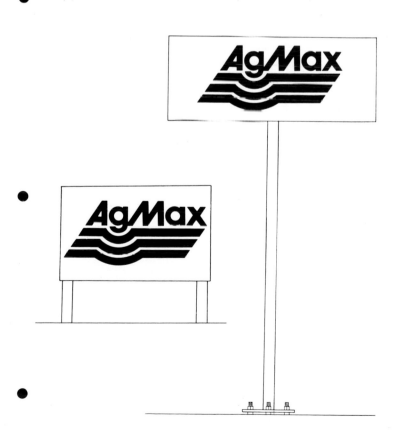

Client American Express Company
Design Firm Communication Services

®

Coordinated signage is important in selling to and servicing the public in countries throughout the world.

Signs and signfaces are usually developed and produced in New York to help reduce costs and maintain quality control. In some cases, a sign may have to be modified locally to meet certain zoning and other local regulations.

Corporate Signs
There are a number of facilities that require corporate signage. The recommended signage for these facilities is the square version of the logotype, which is especially useful for street level display and for flanking doorways. This logotype may be produced in chrome or other metals, if appropriate to the facility.

The horizontal version of the logotype may be utilized if it is more appropriate to the layout or design of the facility. In addition, if appropriate, both the square

and horizontal versions of the logotype may be used in combination on certain facilities.

Travel Office Signs
All signage in American Express Travel Offices has been designed to present and promote a strong, contemporary retail travel image. Whenever possible, Travel Service identification should be in full color.

The blue logotype combined with the visually strong Travel Service mark—with its orange, red and magenta stripes—has become widely recognized by the traveling public. The signage that appears outside the Travel Offices and in both window and interior displays has been designed to include the complete range of travel-related services.

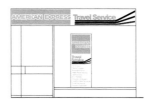

Corporate Signs　　　　　　　　　　　**Travel Office Signs**

Corporate Logotype

The key element in the Company's identification system is the corporate logotype, which also serves as the primary service mark of the Company.

The American Express logotype was designed to be distinctive, contemporary and memorable. In the logotype, the words *American Express* drop out of the blue color background. This American Express Blue is the standard color for the logotype—and as such, it is a vital element in the Company's identification system.

Helvetica Medium—a strong, modern typeface—is the standard typeface recommended for all typography supporting the corporate logotype. Like the blue color, it is readily available worldwide.

Detailed explanations of the logotype, preferred color, background control, supporting typography and official corporate/divisional/subsidiary signatures appear in this section of the Corporate Identification Manual.

Please refer to the *Basic Usage* section whenever communications are being developed.

Note:
Because it's so important to the identification of the Company, the corporate logotype should be used in all communications. To protect the registration of the logotype, the American Express letter forms should not be altered in any way.

Logotype Legal Requirements

The American Express logotype is a registered service mark of American Express Company and its subsidiaries, representatives and other persons having written permission to use it. Permission will be granted only by the Chairman of the Company or his designate. Infringements or unauthorized use should be reported immediately to the General Counsel's office.

Corporate Logotype

---

logotype in colors other than blue or black is not permitted.

Background Color

The preferred application of the blue logotype is on a white background. This background allows for maximum contrast between the American Express letters, the blue field and the white area. Ivory or buff paper—or paper with very light background—may also be used.

When darker backgrounds are necessary, the white version of the logotype may be used. In addition, this version may be used when the logotype is to appear in a continuous color field. The outline version must be used on backgrounds of over 20 percent black.

If you must print the blue logotype on color stock, press adjustments will usually be required to produce a satisfactory match. The blue will tend to vary when blended with the color of the stock.

Supporting Typography

The consistent use of a supporting typestyle serves to strengthen the impression that the travel, financial and insurance services of the Company and its subsidiaries make upon their varied audiences worldwide.

Helvetica is the typeface to be used in all American Express communications—including stationery, business forms, advertising, promotional materials and signage. However, individual advertisements or promotional materials may use other typefaces when specific needs demand it.

The four weights of Helvetica on this page should be given first consideration for use in all graphics. These are available in all type sizes throughout the world.

Light

abcdefghijklmnopqrstuvwxyz
ABCDEFGHIJKLMNOPQRSTUVWXYZ
abcdefghijklmnopqrstuvwxyz
ABCDEFGHIJKLMNOPQRSTUVWXYZ

Regular

abcdefghijklmnopqrstuvwxyz
ABCDEFGHIJKLMNOPQRSTUVWXYZ
abcdefghijklmnopqrstuvwxyz
ABCDEFGHIJKLMNOPQRSTUVWXYZ

Medium

abcdefghijklmnopqrstuvwxyz
ABCDEFGHIJKLMNOPQRSTUVWXYZ
abcdefghijklmnopqrstuvwxyz
ABCDEFGHIJKLMNOPQRSTUVWXYZ

Bold

abcdefghijklmnopqrstuvwxyz
ABCDEFGHIJKLMNOPQRSTUVWXYZ
abcdefghijklmnopqrstuvwxyz
ABCDEFGHIJKLMNOPQRSTUVWXYZ

Background Color Control   Supporting Typography

Client American Heart Association
Designer Gary Hackney
Design Firm American Heart Association

American Heart Association

Newsletters

The use of the signature within newsletter formats and mastheads should be consistent with the guidelines presented in this manual. Revision of existing newsletters that do not reflect correct signature use as presented here should be considered. In newsletters, it is not necessary for text copy and headings to be set in the Helvetica family of type. Mastheads may also be in other typefaces.

Below are examples of newsletter mastheads incorporating correct use of the signature. Design is *not* limited to these, however.

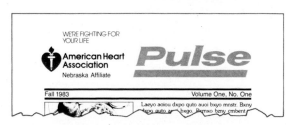

Sizes shown
are reduced.

Signature Configurations

There are seven acceptable configurations of the American Heart Association signature. These configurations have been designed for maximum flexibility and allow for application to various formats.

The symbol of the American Heart Association is a solid red heart, inset with a white torch, and a red flame above. The red used for the heart and flame must be matched by your printer to a color swatch of PMS* 485

(Pantone Matching System — an ink formula available nationwide). White is the preferred background color for the symbol.

*PMS is a standard color matching system copyrighted and trademarked by Pantone, Inc.

One line — Flush left

One line — Flush right

Two line — Flush left

Two line — Flush right

Three line — Flush left

Three line — Flush right

Two line — Centered

Specialty

Specialty items, patches, pins, T-shirts, cards, etc. present unique design problems for any graphic standards program. When possible, every specialty item should follow the specifications, color, signature configuration, etc. presented in this manual.

Shown here are some examples of specialty items and an explanation of how to adapt the guidelines in this manual to their special requirements. Adherence to the guidelines in this manual in all communications pieces will contribute to the "One Heart Association" look and the unified image we are striving to achieve.

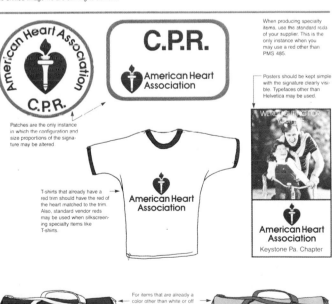

When producing specialty items, use the standard reds of your supplier. This is the only instance when you may use a red other than PMS 485.

Patches are the only instance in which the configuration and size proportions of the signature may be altered

Posters should be kept simple with the signature clearly visible. Typefaces other than Helvetica may be used.

T-shirts that already have a red trim should have the red of the heart matched to the trim. Also, standard vendor reds may be used when silkscreening specialty items like T-shirts.

For items that are already a color other than white or off white, a reverse white signature may be used, or the signature may be matched to a trim color. This is the only instance when deviation from the colors presented on page five is acceptable.

34

Client Atlantic Richfield/Anaconda Industries
Designer Greg Cliff
Design Firm Atlantic Richfield
                   Public Affairs/Design Services

ANACONDA Industries

The Arrowhead

Anaconda Industries has its own symbol, the arrowhead. It is a trademark for various products and also stands for the various divisions. The symbol should be used consistently in all operations that represent Anaconda Industries.

The symbols may appear in black, gray, orange, or white reversed out of gray, black or orange. They may be blind embossed forming a positive shape. They should not be screened, and their shapes should not be used as outlines for other design elements. The symbol must always be reproduced vertically, as shown.

The grid guide shown here can be followed to construct the symbol. However, reproduction quality proofs of the arrowhead shown in the most commonly used sizes are included in the back of this manual.

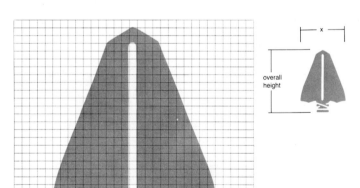

Grid guide

Repeat pattern

Interior Signage

Interior signage must provide direction and identification within Anaconda Industries office buildings and facilities in a manner that enhances each particular design scheme. Therefore, the signs are available in various colors and treatments as described here. Lettering must always be Helvetica Medium or Regular style. For details concerning interior signage, contact the manager of Purchasing in Los Angeles. The five major categories of interior signage include the changeable wall plaque system, desk bars, utility signs, directional signs, and signs applied to glass.

Changeable Wall Plaque Systems

Changeable wall plaques identify semi-private or private offices and specify general use locations. A molded plastic frame contains a removable magnetic vinyl name insert. The basic color is architectural brown with white pressure-sensitive precision die-cut vinyl letters. Among other combinations available, with the approval of the manager of Design Services, are gray with white and chrome with black. There are three types in the wall plaque category.

The name and office number plaque has a 4x4-inch square molded plastic frame with a 4x3-inch upper magnetic vinyl number inset and separate 4x1-inch lower magnetic name inset.

The location plaque displays the number in the upper 4x3-inch inset and the location title in the lower 4x1-inch inset, such as Library, Conference, or File Room.

The executive bar is a polished chrome rectangle with black lettering displaying the executive's name or a location title.

Desk Bars

Desk bars identify employees stationed at desks located in open areas. These bars are prism-shaped, 9 x 2 inches long, and made of polished aluminum with the name applied in black die-cut vinyl lettering.

Utility Signs

Utility signs indicate specific services or functions. Two common utility signs are the elevator label sign and the card reader.

The elevator label sign displays the Company signature and symbol in ¼-inch dimensional brushed aluminum lettering applied directly to the wall surface.

The card reader processes identity cards monitoring the security within a location. The Company signature and symbol is silk-screened on a chrome face plate.

Truck Painting and Marking

A standard scheme of gray and black has been developed for all Company vehicles. Graphic identification shall appear only in the appropriate Company colors. There are no exceptions.

Examples show a series of typical vehicles that cover most variations currently used by the Company. Use those specifications and dimensions on vehicle types noted, and use graphic locations and paint schemes as a guide in determining decal positions and color on vehicle types not shown.

Typical truck cab: Entire chassis and front bumper shall be painted black with cab and wheels in gray. Leave all chrome and natural aluminum unpainted. Company names shall appear in appropriate Company colors or white. All other graphic information shall be in white decals.

Typical van or pickup: Entire chassis, front and rear bumpers and fenders (if separated from cab) shall be painted black, with gray cab, wheels and body. Graphic identifications are located as specified and displayed in appropriate Company colors or white.

Typical semitrailer: Entire chassis shall be painted black, with trailer and wheels painted gray or left unpainted natural aluminum. Company names shall appear in appropriate Company colors or white. All other graphic information shall be in white decals.

Client Columbia Coffee Association
Designers Johannes Regn and Max Phillips
Design Firm Regn/Califano

100% Colombian Coffee ™

Correct Trademark Applications

Unless the trademark developed for 100% Colombian Coffee is used correctly and consistently in package design and promotion, its selling effectiveness will be limited. Using the guidelines set forth in this manual, we have illustrated a series of correct applications of the trademark for your study and packaging guidance.

Positive (black or maroon) trademark on a transparent can lid.

Positive (black or maroon) trademark on a light colored can lid.

Negative (white) trademark on a dark colored can lid.

Positive (black or maroon) trademark on a one-pound, light colored bag.

Negative (white) trademark on a single serving, dark colored package.

Positive (black or maroon) trademark on an advertisement with a light background.

Negative (white) trademark on an advertisement with a dark background.

Negative (white) trademark on a dark colored can.

Positive (black or maroon) trademark on a light colored can.

**Authorized
Trademark Typeface**

The Words "100% Colombian Coffee" in our trademark are set in a typeface known as Typositor Gorilla. A complete alphabet is shown, though it should be readily available from any typesetter. This typeface **must** be used in the trademark, and in order to achieve a coordinated look, you may want to consider using it in your advertising and on your packaging.

Typositor Gorilla

ABCDEFGH
IJKLMNOPQR
STUVWXYZ
abcdefghijklm
nopqrstuvwxyz
1234567890
MRahmntu
ctffffiflffffffThe
()[]*$¢£/%#
@.,.:;!?""''—-

**Authorized Versions
of the Trademark**

The 100% Colombian Coffee trademark has been registered in two versions, positive (black or maroon) and negative (white), and in three colors, black, white, and a rich maroon coffee-hue. To allow maximum design flexibility, choose the alternative that best suits your application. Notice, however, that the negative (white) version is not a simple reverse of the other, but has been redrawn to eliminate the dark skin, white eyes and "snow-covered" mountain that otherwise would result.

The positive (maroon or black) versions of the trademark are ideally suited to light-

colored backgrounds, whereas the negative (white) version is designed for dark backgrounds.

Please don't reverse the trademark photographically. This is not authorized, because the result will not have a pleasing appearance.

Trademark size is also important. Experience shows that in reductions below 11/16" (17mm) the details become unrecognizable, and the type is almost impossible to read. In order for the trademark to be truly effective for you, don't use a smaller size than provided in this manual.

Positive Version (Black and Maroon)

Negative Version (White)

Client Planned Parenthood Federation
of America, Inc.
Designers Ellen Sickle, David Svet,
David Cooke
Design Firm Design Collective Incorporated

Planned Parenthood®
Federation of America, Inc.

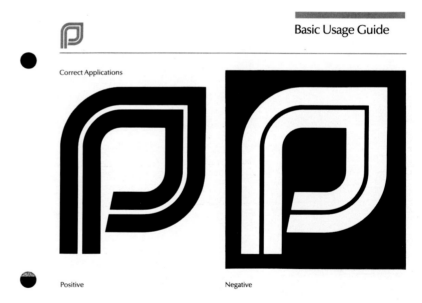

Basic Usage Guide

Correct Applications

Positive

Negative

The logo may be used as positive or
negative artwork.
  When using a positive logo, use a
positive signature. When using a
negative logo, use a negative signature.
  The logo must always be placed up-
right, never at an angle or upside
down.
  The logo may appear alone, without
the signature. However, the signature may never appear without the
logo.
  The logo is always measured by the
height rather than the width.
  Refer to Section 11—"Production

Notes" for ink color recommenda-
tions.

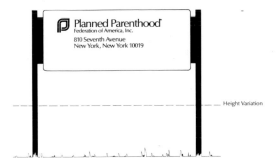

Height Variation

This illustration shows an example of a freestanding, post mounted, exterior sign.

The important consideration in developing exterior signage is to maintain the logo and legal signature in their proper position, in proportion with the rest of the identity program.

The logo and legal signature can appear with or without the address. Refer to Basic Usage Guide—Section 1 —"Logo and Legal Signature" for proper positioning.

The freestanding signage can be manufactured from various materials. The sign can be constructed from wood, plastic, extruded aluminum, steel or a composition fiber product.

The dotted line indicates height variation. The freestanding sign can be manufactured short or tall depending upon the needs of the affiliate.

There are many options in designing signage. How the sign is mounted will be determined by the affiliate's needs, budget and the signage laws of the community. Color, size and position will also be determined after considering the many variables in sign manufacturing. Depending upon the substance, the sign can be illuminated either externally or internally.

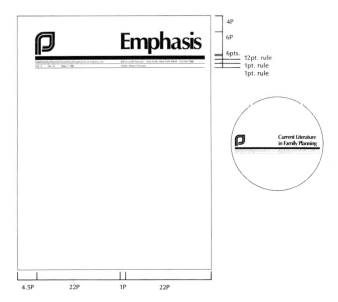

4P
6P
6pts.   12pt. rule
             1pt. rule
             1pt. rule

Current Literature
in Family Planning

4.5P   22P   1P   22P

In order to create artwork for a newsletter, follow this example.

The newsletter is always to be 8½" x 11" in size.

The page can be divided into 2 columns with a 4.5 pica left margin.

Each column is 22 picas wide with 1 pica between columns.

The page could also be divided into 3 columns with a 4.5 pica left margin.

Each column is 14 picas 3 pts. wide with 1 pica between columns.

The rules along with the logo are flush left at this 4.5 pica measurement. Place the logo 4.5 picas from the left edge of the page.

Make certain that the baseline or bottom of the logo is 10 picas from the top of the page.

The logo itself should be 6 picas high.

The signature will not appear on the newsletter.

There are 6 pts. between the bottom of the logo and the top of the 12 pt. rule.

The 12 pt. rule extends 45 picas.

There is 12 pt. spacing between the 12 pt. rule and the 1 pt. rule.

There is a 12 pt. space following the 1 pt. rule and then another 1 pt. rule.

The type between the rules is 8 pt. Optima Medium.

The title is flush with the second column and is in 72 pt. Optima Bold with tight kerning.

The detail shows a stacked title in 36 pt. Optima Bold type, with tight kerning.

Both the division heading and the address line are flush left with the newsletter heading.

The newsletter should always be printed with a dark ink color and light paper.

Consideration needs to be given to

Client Rocky Mountain Child Health Services
Designers Duane Wiens, Carl Baden
Arvid Wallen
Design Firm Matrix International, Inc.

Rocky Mountain Child Health Services

Logo

Rocky Mountain Child Health Services recognizes the importance of consistent, memorable identification of its facilities, personnel and services, and has adopted the logo reproduced below. To achieve consistency, certain guidelines for usage and presentation are essential. The information which follows is designed to assist in material creation, coordination and production.

Because effective identification relies upon simple, visually clear statements, ample background space around the logo and name is mandatory. With the same reasoning, the logo

should never be hand drawn or otherwise distorted by the addition of block of color, ornamentation, distracting shapes, use of texture, or by screening.

A certificate of registration for our logo symbol from the United States Patent Trademark Office has been received.

Logo Grid

Reproducing the logo accurately, regardless of the finished size or reproduction technique, is extremely important in a graphics identity program. The logo sheets provided will satisfy most normal requirements, but exceptions will undoubtedly arise over the course of time. In these instances, camera enlargement or reduction of the finished art is preferred. When the end use (such as large signage projects) make this method impossible, the logo grid drawing will be helpful.

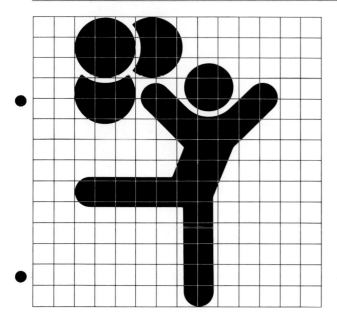

Logo and Names

To ensure continuity and enhance recognition, the graphic identification for each division of Rocky Mountain Child Health Services and designated subsidiaries consists of the primary logo with the specific division name in Helvetica Regular. The two elements combine to create an easy to use, balanced visual unit.

For further explanation of usage of the logo and names, refer to the logo and graphic integrity policy.

The preferred arrangement of these elements is shown below, and changes from this format are discouraged. The name and logo should not be centered except in those special circumstances when a centered format is used, (e.g., an advertisement with centered copy).

The name spacing is considered part of the design. Therefore it is necessary for only supplied proofs to be used for reproduction. The logo should not be hand drawn, and the name should not appear in any other type style except when it is used as part of the text copy.

Rocky Mountain
Child Health Services

The Children's Hospital
Foundation

The Children's Hospital

Client Sentry Hardware
Design Firm Babcock & Schmid
Associates, Inc.

Stationery | Mailing Labels

There are two approved versions of mailing labels. The **corporate** label is used by Sentry Hardware Corporation. Any distributor/dealer who prefers this format may adopt it by using his own name and address. The second version is for use by **distributors/dealers** only. A strong emphasis has been placed on your company name.

Mailing labels should be printed in the three Sentry colors, or in just one of the Sentry colors, if desired. Refer to page 1|6, Section 1. A printed typing dot insures correct placement of typed copy. [Typing dots indicate base line of typewritten copy]. Mailing labels may have rounded corners.

Specifications:
Company Name:
  Corporate: 8/9 pt. Helvetica Medium
  Distributor/Dealer: 14 pt. Helvetica Medium
Address: 8/9 pt. Helvetica Regular
Other Copy: 12 pt. Helvetica Regular or
  Medium, depending on emphasis
Color: Sentry Red, Sentry Blue, Black
Paper: White, coated

Corporate

Distributor/Dealer

Depending on where it is placed, the trademark faces right or left and will be referred to as **sentry right face** or **sentry left face** where it is necessary to distinguish between the two. The preferred version is sentry right face.

Usage rule. The trademark must always face into any given area, never toward an edge or margin. The trademark must always face any graphic element or copy that is adjacent to it. If the trademark is centered in any given area, it must always face right.

The only acceptable size relationship between the symbol [pictorial sentry] and the logotype [word Sentry] is shown below by units "X" and "Y". Exceptions are signage and vehicle identification, which are strictly controlled by Sentry Hardware Corporation.

Preferred
Sentry Right Face

X equals the thickness of the horizontal strokes of the letters in the logotype [word Sentry].

Y equals the width of the symbol [pictorial sentry].

Sentry Left Face

Additional trademark format information on page 1|3, this section.

Note the diagonal line may bleed off the right side of the card if it bisects the Sentry Identification Band at one half the width of the package.

Examples

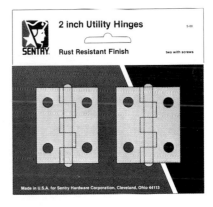

Client The Sherwin Williams Company
Design Firm Babcock & Schmid
Associates, Inc.

416

A suggested format has been
developed in order to establish
consistency in the typing of all
Sherwin-Williams letterheads and
envelopes.

All copy will appear flush left and
ragged right with paragraphs
separated by a space. In order to

Typing Format

facilitate the positioning of the copy,
small tic marks have been printed to
indicate the placement of the address
and body copy on the letterhead, the
body copy on the second sheet, and
name and address on the envelope.

Name, title and signature also appear
flush left as indicated in the
example below.

Typography and
Spacing System

Univers 65, illustrated below, is used
in all signage. In order to ensure
consistent legibility and appearance
on all signs, a system has been

developed establishing a formula for
inter-letter and word spacing. A
complete spacing system may be
obtained through the Corporate
Identification Department.

UNIVERS 65

ABCDEFGHIJKLMNOPQRSTUVWXY
ZÆŒØ 1234567890
abcdefghijklmnopqrstuvwxyzæœø

A Spacing
System Pro

Retail Storefront
Identity Signs 40′
and Over (5′ Sign Height)

Additional formulas determining color
spectrum proportions have been
established to accommodate those
storefront having dimensions 40′

and over. Graphics for sign heights
other than 5′ (i.e., 3′ and 4′) are
proportionately determined.
In order to have more presence on
sign lengths 40′ and over, the
corporate symbol is modified as

illustrated below. This represents the
only situation where modification
of the corporate symbol occurs. A
grid overlay for accurate enlargement
in reproduction is available through
the Store Planning Department.

Specifications
Symbol : White on a corporate blue background
Spectrum colors : Spectrum magenta, spectrum red,
  spectrum orange, spectrum yellow
Sign face material : Vacuum-formed acrylic,
  sub-surface printed
Frame : Extruded aluminum, natural finish
Illumination : Optional
Mounting : Flush-mounted to wall

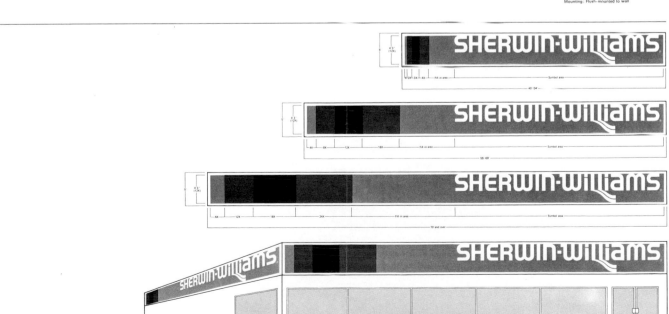

Client United Technologies Corporation
Designers Hans Peter Weiss, Gunther Maier
Design Firm GGK New York Advertising

LOOK HOW WE LOOK.

Each of the Electronics Sector's companies now runs its own ads. With its own budget. In its own media. Our efforts never combine. Together we spend a huge budget, but we don't project the image of a huge group. The impression we leave on our audiences is like this disorganized bunch of ads. If the dozen companies of the Electronics Sector would rally together, the Sector — and each of its members — would suddenly have one big, ongoing program.

To do this, we will use a single style in all our advertising. Here's how we'll go about it.

3

GOUDY OLD STYLE FOR THE COPY.

The typeface for all body copy is Goudy Old Style. Every typesetter has it. It is a serif typeface with a very full and light cut.

The regular size is 20 pt. over 20 pt. There is no line leading. It should be set in block, flush right and left. Each paragraph, including the first one, starts with an indent of one em-quad. Normally the indent would also be 20 pt. The typical size ad, as shown in the beginning of this book, would then run 18 lines deep and 33 picas wide. That means roughly 970 characters (including punctuation and spacing), or about 140 words.

Uhdgdr vcfcd czxzsd fdrdt gftfy hgygu jhkh mnknl ko, sawae dsc fdrdt gftfy hgygj eqwa xzszd cxv. Mgdfdr fsde ewre tryr utyy kjijo lkokp dasw, vzczx dsesrd. Wdse fdgd hfjf gmgj jhuhi kkjljo lkoko kjij.

Ahfgfb vcf bcgkghcf fdrdt gflkokptfy hgygu jhui kjio kjbxcxdsljolj mnjn nvbvgv vcfcdx czxzdsesr fdrdr

Let's say you have to write about a subject that demands more than 140 words. Then you simply use a smaller point size. Let's say 18 pt. or 16 pt. But don't set type any smaller than 14 pt. If you use 14 pt., the block of type would be the equivalent of one single-spaced typewritten page.

Malskkd apoie aoidioa se jkdl; alksjd ooqieiduc nfd sakender mitenterim inqwer oasiduf klf mknjbhv djsueu sjsdkfjgh aosieurjd nwhweyd

Malskkd apoie aoidioa se jkdl; alksjd ooqieiduc nfd sakender mitenterim inqwer oasiduf klf mknjbhv djsueu sjsdkfjgh aosieurjd nwhweyd alkd aldme. Solwee ossieud kdd koji dssndbdgrt ssyeyd zmfhffhvk-owieir isd amdnf — formen wsedbf msjejudy sjdjflv. Solendb dkjf ujegdtf dan olwdkfj asjdnb saskenten vanden knjbhv djsueu sjskoijgh aosieurjd nwhweyd amkd aldme. Sonwe osieud kdd koji dssndbdgrt ssyeydal zmfhhanvk-owieir isd

Malskkd apoie aoidioa se jkdl; alksjd ooqieiduc nfd sakender mitenterim inqwer oasiduf klf mknjbhv djsueu sjsdkfjgh aosieurjd nwhweyd alkd aldme. Solwee ossieud kdd koji dssndbdgrt ssyeyd zmfhffhvk-owieir isd amdnf — formen wsedbf msjejudy sjdjflv. Solendb dkjf ujegdtf dan olwdkfj asjdnb saskenten vanden knjbhv djsueu sjskoijgh aosieurjd nwhweyd amkd aldme. Sonwe osieud kdd koji dssndbdgrt ssyeydal zmfhhanvk-owieir isd amoeiru formen wsedbf

Malskkd apoie aoidioa se jkdl; alksjd ooqieiduc nfd sakender mitenterim inqwer oasiduf klf mknjbhv djsueu sjsdkfjgh aosieurjd nwhweyd alkd aldme. Solwee ossieud kdd koji dssndbdgrt ssyeyd zmfhffhvk-owieir isd amdnf — formen wsedbf msjejudy sjdjflv. Solendb dkjf ujegdtf dan olwdkfj asjdnb saskenten vanden knjbhv djsueu sjskoijgh aosieurjd

BOLD FOR EMPHASIS.

If you want to emphasize some words, or designate paragraphs, use **Goudy Extra Bold** in the same point size as your running copy. Be very careful when using this heavier typeface. Too much will distort your ad. At worst it will be **unreadable** and compete with the illustration.

Uhdgdr vcfcd czxzsd fdrdt gftfy hgygu jhkh mnknl kjio kjbxcxdsljolj mnjn nvbvgv vcfcdx czxzdsesr fdrdr ko, sawae dsc fdrdt gftfy hgygj eqwa xzszd cxv. Mgdfdr fsde ewre tryr utyy kjijo lkokp dasw, vzczx dsesrd. Wdse fdgd hfjf gmgj jhuhi kkjljo lkoko kjij.

Goudy vcf bcgkghcf fdrdt gflkokptfy hgygu jhui kjio kjbxcxdsljolj mnjn nvbvgv vcfcdx czxzdsesr fdrdr sawae dsesr fdcxvc vcfcg bvgvh. **Extra** hgjg mbnbj khih khiho kjljo khjhu nbb vcd cxdxf czxzs dsesr fdrdt.

Ncxdx dswse dsesr **Bold** gftfy hgygug jhklhkh mbnbh bcvcf cxdxs xzszw dsesrf fdrdt gftfr vzczx

If you want to emphasize some words, or designate paragraphs, use the **Goudy Extra Bold** in the same point size as your running copy. Be very careful when using this heavier typeface. **Too much will distort** your ad. At worst it will be unreadable and compete with the illustration.

Ahfgfb vcf begkghcf fdrdt gflkokptfy hgygu jhui kjio kjbxcxdsljolj mnjn nvbvgv vcfcdx czxzdsesr fdrdt sawae dsesr fdcxvc eqwa xzszd cxv. **Too much will distort** kjijo lkokp dasw, vzczx dsesrd. Wdse fdgd hfjf gmgj jhuhi kkjljo lkoko kjij.

Ahfgfb vcf bcgkghcf fdrdt gflkokptfy hgygu jhui kjio kjbxcxdsljolj mnjn nvbvgv vcfcdx czxzdsesr fdrdt sawae dsesr fdcxvc vcfcg bvgvh. Bgftfy hgjg mbnbj khih khiho kjljo khjhu nbb vcd cxdxf czxzs dsesr fdrdt.

In case you really hav gftfy hgygug jhklhkh mbnbh bcvcf cxdxs xzszw dsesrf fdrdt gftfr vzczx sawaed dsfsde fdedr gftfy **Too much will distort uch will distort** fdgdt gfbvgf nbhgjgk mnjnkh jhuy ponvbvg gdfdt.

Uhdgdr vcfcd czxzsd fdrdt gftfy hgygu jhkh mnknl ko, sawae dsc fdrdt gftfy hgygj eqwa xzszd cxv. **Goudy Extra Bold** r utyy kjijo lkokp dasw, vzczx dsesrd. Wdse fdgd hfjf gmgj jhuhi kkjljo lkoko kjij.

Ncxdx dswse dsesr fdrdt gftfy hgygug jhklhkh mbnbh bcvcf cxdxs xzszw dsesrf fdrdt gftfr vzczx sawaed dsfsde fdedr gftfy jhklhkh mbnbh bcvcf cxdxs xzszw dsesr

Uhdgdr vcfcd czxzsd fdrdt gftfy hgygu jhkh mnknl ko, sawae dsc fdrdt gftfy hgygj eqwa xzszd cxv. **In case you really have** kjijo lkokp dasw, vzczx dsesrd. Wdse fdgd hfjf gmgj jhuhi kkjljo lkoko kjij.

Ahfgfb vcf bcgkghcf fdrdt gflkokptfy hgygu jhui kjio kjbxcxdsljolj mnjn nvbvgv vcfcdx czxzdsesr fdrdt sawae dsesr fdcxvc vcfcg bvgvl. Bgftfy hgjg mbnhj khih khiho kjljo khjhu nbb vcd cxdxf czxzs dsesr fdrdt.

Ncxdx dswse dsesr fdrdt gftfy hgygug jhklhkh mbnbh bcvcf cxdxs xzszw dsesrf **In case you really have** fsde fdedr gftfy hgjgu nbjbu khihokm brvcxd sawae dsesr fdgdt gfbvgf nbhgjgk mnjnkh jhuy ponvbvg gdfdt.

Uhdgdr vcfcd czxzsd fdrdt gftfy hgygu jhkh mnknl ko, sawae dsc fdrdt gftfy hgygj eqwa xzszd cxv. 'Mgdfdr **Goudy Extra Bol** kjijo lkokp dasw, vzczx dsesrd. Wdse fdgd hfjf gmgj jhuhi kkjljo lkoko kjij.

Ncxdx dswse dsesr fdrdt gftfy hgygug jhklhkh **In case you really have** dsesrf fdrdt gftfr vzczx sawaed dsfsde fdedr gftfy **much will distort m** brvcxd sawae dsesr fdgdt gfbvgf nbhgjgk mnjnkh jhuy ponvbvg gdfdt.

Uhdgdr vcfcd czxzsd fdrdt gftfy hgygu jhkh mnknl ko, sawae dsc fdrdt gftfy hgygj eqwa xzszd cxv. Mgdfdr fsde ewre tryr utyy kjijo lkokp dasw, vzcz **Goudy Extra Bold** hfjf gmgj jhuhi kkjljo lkoko kjij gftfy hgygug fdrdt gftfr vzczx sawaed dsfsde fdedr gftfy

Client Westin Hotels-Property
Designers John Hornall, Jack Anderson,
Rey Sabado
Design Firm John Hornall Design Works

WESTIN HOTELS

4C

Check, Standard

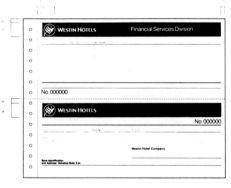

The standard check
follows the format shown.
The format may be
adapted for computer and
bank systems.

The corporate signature is
printed in the horizontal
version.

Specifications

Type: "Westin Hotel
Company", Helvetica Bold,
10 pt. "PAY", Helvetica
Light, 10 pt. Other copy,
Helvetica Light and Bold,
8 pt.

Mailing Label

The mailing label is used for large envelopes, packages, etc. It has a gummed back and is suitable for all classes of mail.

Special instructions to the post office are not necessary except for return or forwarding information on third or fourth class mail.

The same format should be used for continuous form labels, although size may be altered if necessary.

Specifications

Size: 5" x 3"

Stock: White

Type: Address line, Helvetica Light, 8 pt.

Ink color: Westin gray

Envelope, Monarch

Shown 45% of actual size; actual size is 7½" x 3⅞".

The regular Monarch envelope should be printed on the same stock and in the same colors as the Monarch letterhead.

The signature format is the same for regular and Air Mail envelopes.

The Air Mail format, which is shown on the bottom example, is recommended for mail sent outside the United States, Canada and Mexico.

The rule line must bleed off the right side. This can be insured by printing envelopes prior to folding, with rule line extending ⅛" beyond the fold line.

Specifications

Size: 7½" x 3⅞"

Type: Address line, Helvetica Light, 8 pt. Air Mail identification, Helvetica Light, 14 pt.

Ink color: Same as letterhead. Air Mail envelope, "Air Mail", blue; Air Mail bars, Westin wine and blue.

Client Westin Hotels
Designers John Hornall, Jack Anderson
Design Firm John Hornall Design Works

WESTIN HOTELS

1R

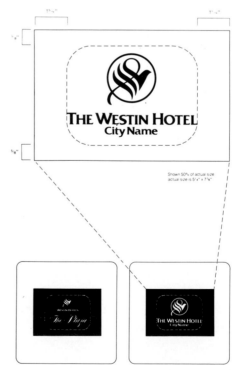

**Radio/Television
Advertising**

In radio and television
commercials, hotels
without Westin in the name
should include Westin
identification in the audio
portion of the spot. For
example, "The Plaza, a
Westin Hotel."

For all hotels, visual
identification should be
included in television
commercials longer than
ten seconds.

The examples show art-
work and a reduction to a
35mm slide format for a
hotel with Westin in the
property name (left) and a
hotel without Westin in the
name (far left).

The format is also suitable
for television and video
tape presentations.

The property signature
should be displayed on the
last frame of the
commercial. The back-
ground should be a solid
color. The signature should
appear in one color only, as
large as possible within the
designated area, as
shown.

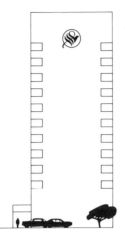

On top of a high tower or narrow building, the full signature may not be legible from the street level. These signs should display the corporate symbol only, as shown.

Note: All building exterior signing plans must be submitted to the Director of Advertising and Public Relations, Marketing Division, who will obtain the necessary approvals. See the procedure for submitting plans on page 1 of this section, Signs, Building Exterior.

Drive-through canopy entrances should display hotel identification on the side facing the traffic flow. Identification may be used on two opposite sides of the entrance. Avoid identification on adjacent sides of the entrance.

These signs should use the full property signature, when possible.

Note: All building exterior signing plans must be submitted to the Director of Advertising and Public Relations, Marketing Division, who will obtain the necessary approvals. See the procedure for submitting plans on page 1 of this section, Signs, Building Exterior.

Corporate Marks

Client Abbott Laboratories
Designer George Nelson
Design Firm George Nelson and Co., Inc.

Client Aetna Insurance Co.
Designer Andrew R. Giarnella
Design Firm Giarnella Design

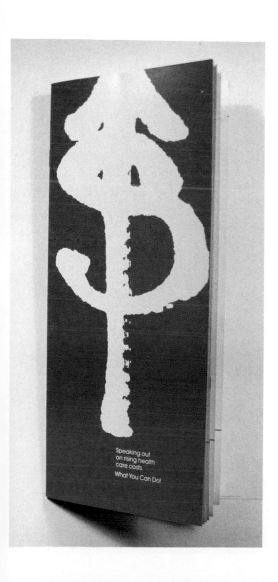

Speaking out
on rising health
care costs.

What You Can Do!

Client Akron Art Museum
Design Firm Babcock & Schmid
Associates, Inc.

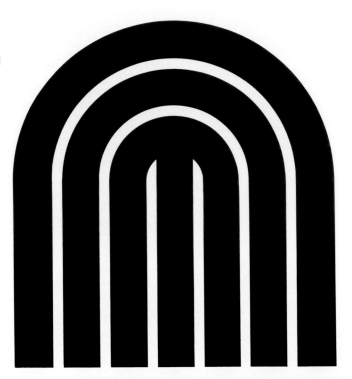

Client Aladdin Travel
Designer Stavros Cosmopulos
Design Firm Cosmopulos, Crowley & Daly

WANT SAMOA?

Fiji? Tahiti? St. Martin? Aruba? Bermuda? Aladdin cruises the seven seas. Aladdin can take you wherever your imagination wants to go. Tell your Aladdin Travel Consultant exactly what you want. We have enough cruises to please everyone. Call Aladdin today. We can make your most exotic cruise dreams come true.

ACAPULCO	from $399⁰⁰	FREEPORT/GRAND BAHAMA	from $199⁰⁰
ST. MAARTEN	from $399⁰⁰	ORLANDO	from $199⁰⁰
ARUBA	from $399⁰⁰	BARBADOS	from $399⁰⁰
NASSAU/PARADISE ISLAND	from $219⁰⁰	ANTIGUA	from $399⁰⁰

All vacations include round trip jet air fare, hotel accommodations, round trip transfers and baggage handling. Optional meal plans available.

All prices are based on per person double occupancy, plus applicable taxes and service, and vary by departure date and length of stay.

In Swampscott and at seven Filene's locations:
212 Humphrey Street, Swampscott/ 598-5820 • **Filene's** 426 Washington Street, Boston/357-2178 • **Filene's** South Shore Plaza, Braintree/848-0511

WE'RE WITH YOU ALL THE WAY.

• **Filene's** Burlington Mall/272-3439
• **Filene's** The Mall at Chestnut Hill/ 965-5580 • **Filene's** Natick Mall/ 653-0401 • **Filene's** North Shore Shopping Center, Peabody/532-1166
• **Filene's** Worcester Center/752-2419

Client American Savings Bank
Designer Alan Peckolick
Design Firm Lubalin Peckolick

Client Ameritech
Designer Goldsholl Associates
Design Firm Goldsholl Associates

AMERITECH

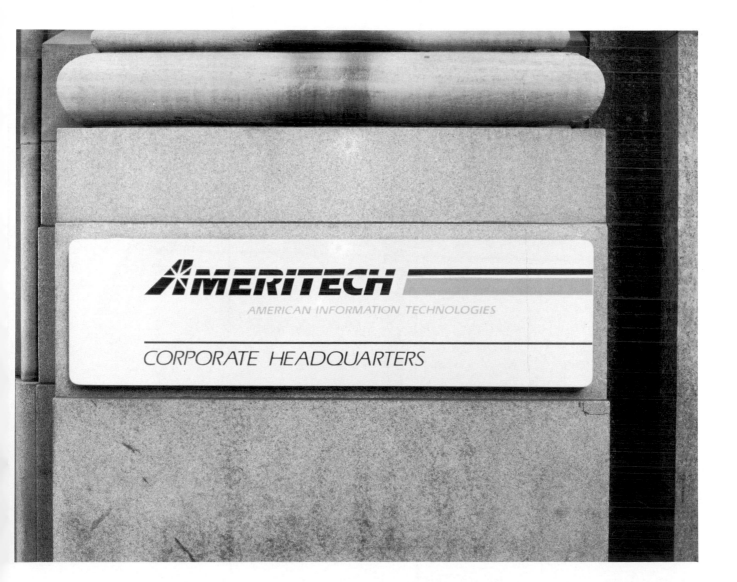

Client Arkwright-Interlaken, Inc.
Design Firm Malcolm Grear Designers, Inc.

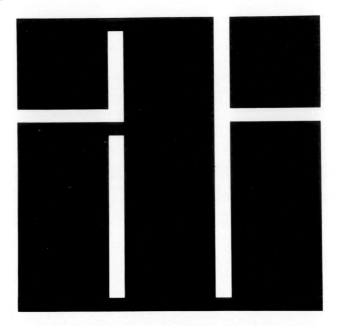

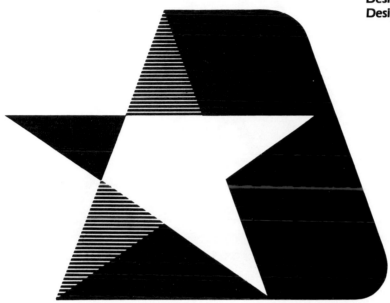

Client Armour & Company
Designer Marketing Design Group
Design Firm Landor Associates

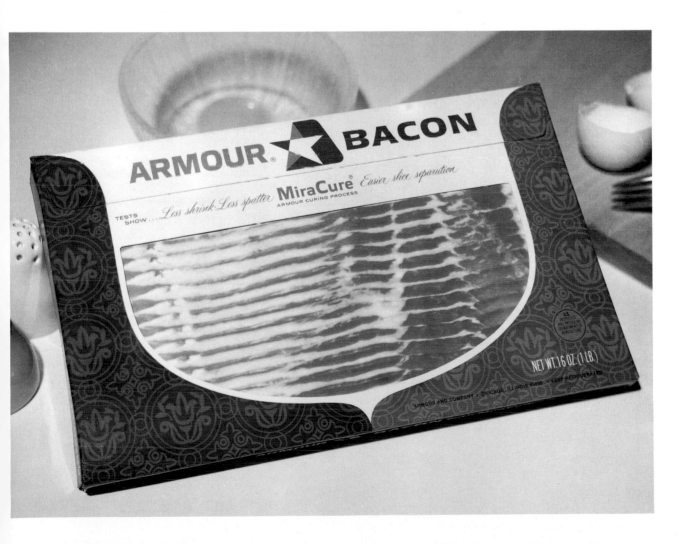

Client Artist Foundation
Designer Tom Demeter
Design Firm Cosmopulos, Crowley & Daly

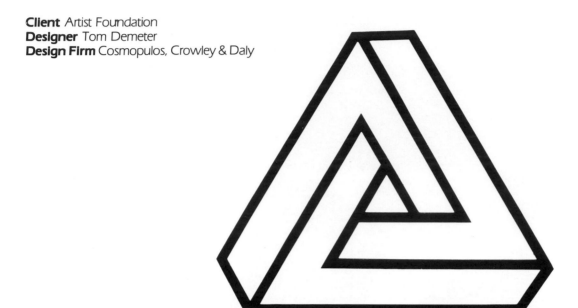

ART ON ICE.

The Artists Foundation is proud to sponsor tonight's game between Harvard University and The 1984 Olympic Hockey Team. We are pleased to be able to support the Olympic Team in their pursuit of excellence. The Gold Medal. For the past ten years, The Artists Foundation has been pursuing excellence in the arts by providing professional and financial support to professional artists.

The Artists Foundation, Inc.
110 Broad Street, Boston, Massachusetts 02110   Telephone: (617) 482-8100

Client Asbury United Methodist Church
Designer John K. Landis
Design Firm John K. Landis Graphic Design

asbury united methodist church

Client Atlanta International Airport
Designer Steven B. Rousso
Design Firm Garrett/Lewis/Johnson

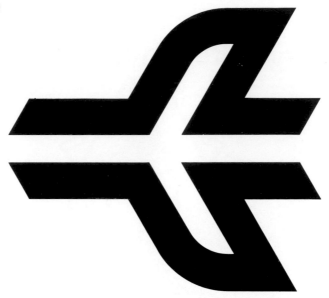

Client Banana Republic
Designers Primo Angeli, Eric Read
Design Firm Primo Angeli Graphics

Client Bankers Fund
Designers Tom Demeter
Design Firm Cosmopulos, Crowley & Daly

BANKERS FUND™

A BETTER
MARKET
FOR
YOUR
MONEY

LOWELL INSTITUTION
BANKERS FUND™
★ FOR SAVINGS ★

Client Boston Breakers
Designer Tom Demeter
Design Firm Cosmopulos, Crowley & Daly

Client Brier Manufacturing
Designer Malcolm Grear Designers, Inc.
Design Firm Malcolm Grear Designers, Inc.

Client Brookfield Zoo
Designers Tamar Rosenthal,
Hannah Jennings (Art Director)
Design Firm Brookfield Zoo

Client Brown University Press
Designer Malcolm Grear Designers, Inc.
Design Firm Malcolm Grear Designers, Inc.

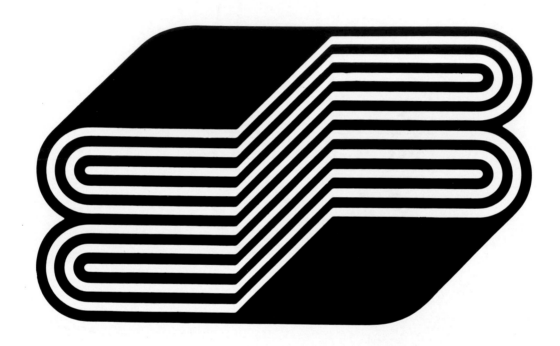

Client Bruce Hands
Designers Jack Anderson, Cliff Chung
Design Firm John Hornall Design Works

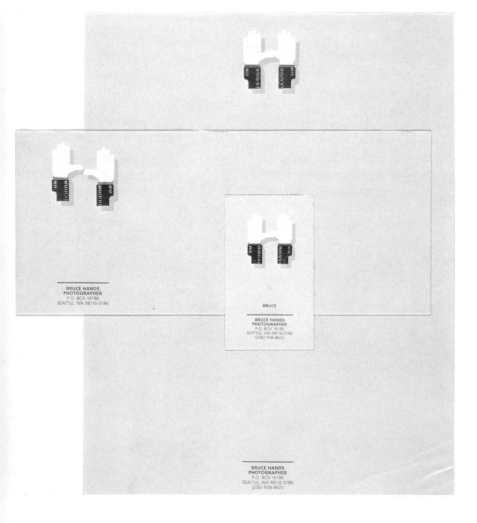

Client Cardiac Wellness Games
Designers Deanna Wassom,
        Mike Herburger
Design Firm Wayfairer

Cardiac ♥ Wellness ♥ Games

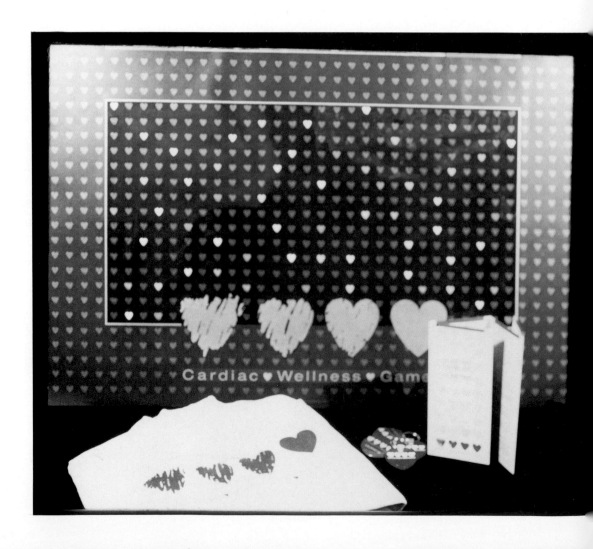

Client Caspian Caviar
Designer Milton Glaser
Design Firm Milton Glaser Inc.

Client Castle and Cooke
Designers Primo Angeli, Mark Jones,
　　　　　Ray Honda
Design Firm Primo Angeli Graphics

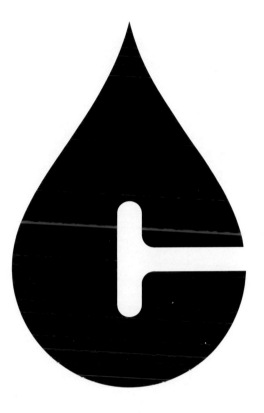

Client Central Florida Blood Bank
Designer Joe Bailey
Design Firm McAllister-Barker Associates

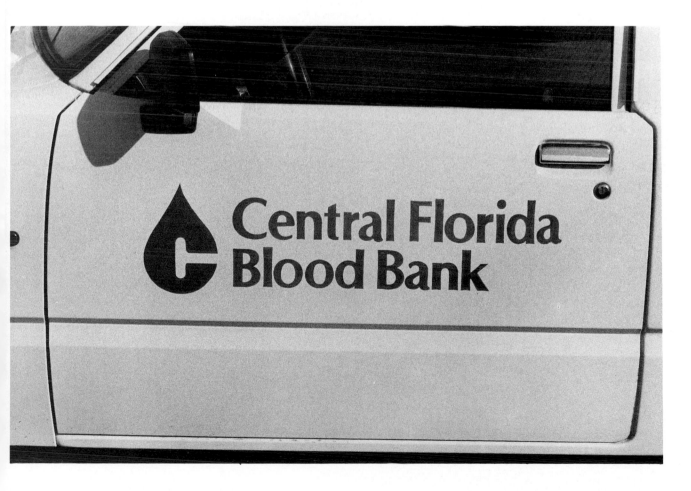

Client WCVB-TV, Channel 5, Boston
Designers Lance Wyman, Bill Cannan
Design Firm Wyman & Cannan Co., Ltd.

Client Chemical Bank
Designer Erick DeMartino
Design Firm DeMartino/Schultz Inc.

Client Chiba Bank (Tokyo, Japan)
Designer Lee & Young Communications
Design Firm Lee & Young Communications

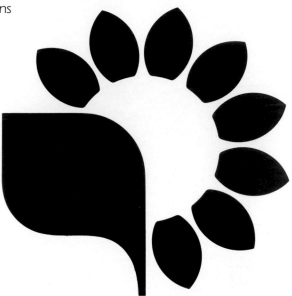

CHICAGO SYMPHONY ORCHESTRA

Client Chicago Symphony Orchestra
Designer Gini Kondziolka
Design Firm Kondziolka Takatsuki Design

Client Arron Cushman Associates
Chicago White Sox
Designer Daniel Bernstein
Design Firm The Daniel Bernstein Design
Group, Inc.

SCHEDULE

AUGUST						
1 California	2	3 * Oakland	4 * Oakland	5	6 * Kansas City	7 * Kansas City
8 * DH Kansas City	9 N Cleveland	10	11 * N Cleveland	12	13 N Baltimore	14 * TN Baltimore
15 * Baltimore	16 Boston	17 * Boston	18 * Boston	19	20 * Baltimore	21 * Baltimore
22 * DH Baltimore	23 N Detroit	24 * N Detroit	25 * N Detroit	26	27 * Milwaukee	28 * Milwaukee
29 * Milwaukee	30	31 * Cleveland				

SEPTEMBER						
		1 * Cleveland	2	3 * N Minnesota	4 * Minnesota	
5 * *Minnesota	6 11 AM Minnesota	7 N Oakland	8 N Oakland	9 Oakland	10 * California	11 * California
12 * DH California	13 * Kansas City	14 * Kansas City	15 * Texas	16 * Texas	17 N Kansas City	18 N Kansas City
19 Kansas City	20	21 * Minnesota	22 * Minnesota	23 * Minnesota	24 * Oakland	25 * Oakland
26 * Oakland	27	28	29 N California	30 N California	OCT 1 N Texas	OCT 2 N Texas
OCT 3 Texas						

Away *T.V. games WSNS-44. All games WMAQ Radio 67.
Home Games Day 1:15 P.M. (July 3, 10:00 A.M.)
Night Games 8:00 P.M.
Doubleheader 12:30 P.M.
Box seats: $4.50;   Reserved seats: $3.50
General Admission: $2.00   Parking: $2.00
Senior Citizens half price on April 11, June 20,
July 18 & 21, August 21, September 14 & 16.
All family members half price (all seats) on April 27,
May 22, June 30, July 15, August 7.
All teens half price (all seats) on April 30, June 4, July 1.

Client Children's Museum
Designer Stavros Cosmopulos
Design Firm Cosmopulos, Crowley & Daly

Client Cine-Graphis
Designer Lauren Smith
Design Firm Lauren Smith Design

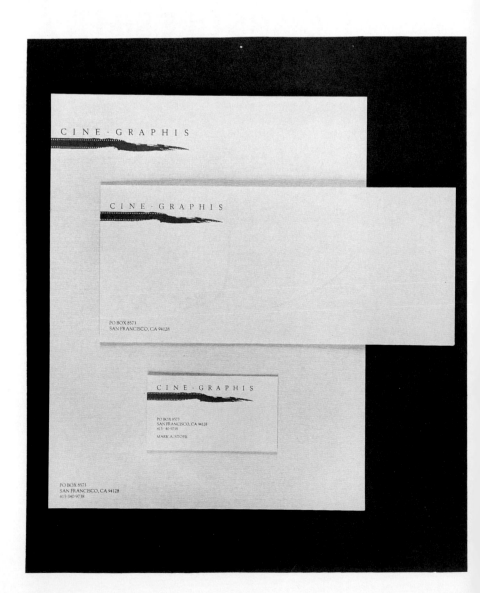

Client Circular Screen,
    Commercial Silk Screen Printer
Designer John K. Landis
Design Firm John K. Landis Graphic Design

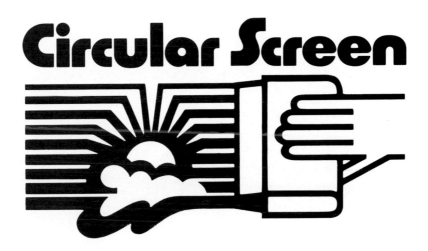

Client City of St. Petersburg
Designer Ron Whitney
Design Firm City of St. Petersburg
Marketing/Public Information

CITY OF ST. PETERSBURG

Client Cole Film Service
Designers Michael Waitsman,
Liane Sebastian
Design Firm Synthesis Concepts, Inc.

 cole film service, inc.

740 NORTH RUSH
SUITE 611
CHICAGO, IL 60611
312/787-7624

Client Compton Advertising
Designer Peter McGuggart
Design Firm Compton Advertising

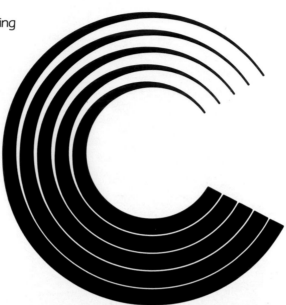

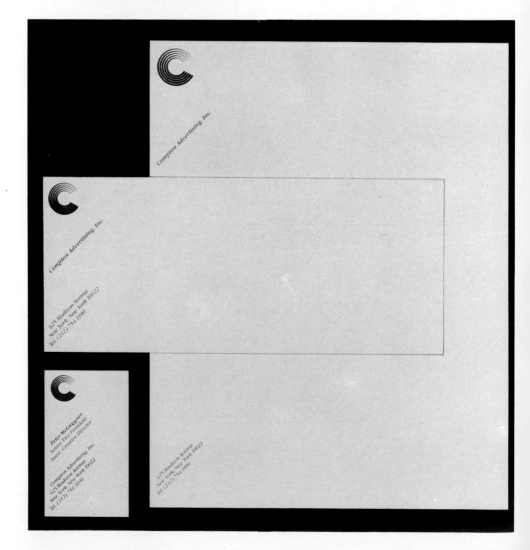

Client Continental Express
Designer David O. Wright
Design Firm Creative Works

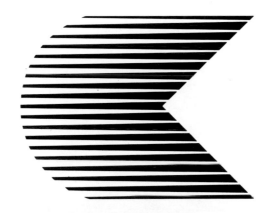

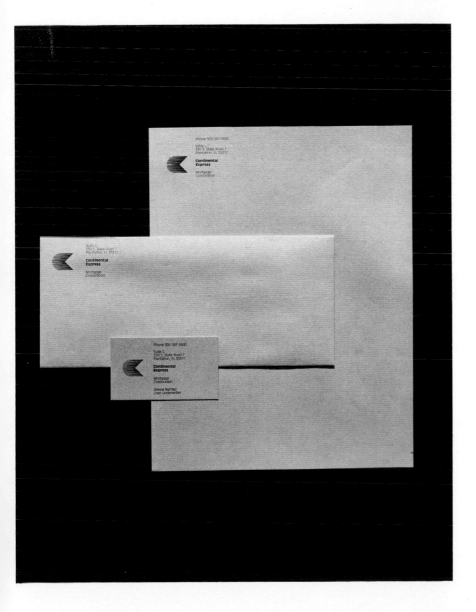

Client Corvus Systems
Designers Howard York (Creative Director),
Dale Brock (Project Design Dir.)
Design Firm S&O Consultants

Client Cotton Inc.
Design Firm Landor Associates

Client Data General
Designer Stavros Cosmopulos
Design Firm Cosmopulos, Crowley & Daly

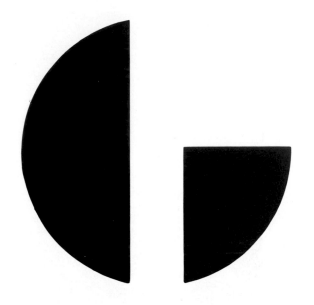

Client DP (Design Productions)
Designer Marco DePlano
Design Firm Marco DePlano & Associates

9"

Reflective Material

Client Downtown Orlando, Inc.
Designer Joe Bailey
Design Firm Joe Bailey: Advertising by Design

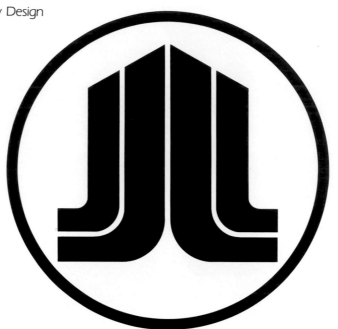

Client Dr. Pepper Company
Designer C.M. Seminario
Design Firm The Berni Corporation

Client Dynascan Corp.-Cobra Division
Designers Richard Wittosch, Jane Urban
Design Firm Contours Consulting
Design Group

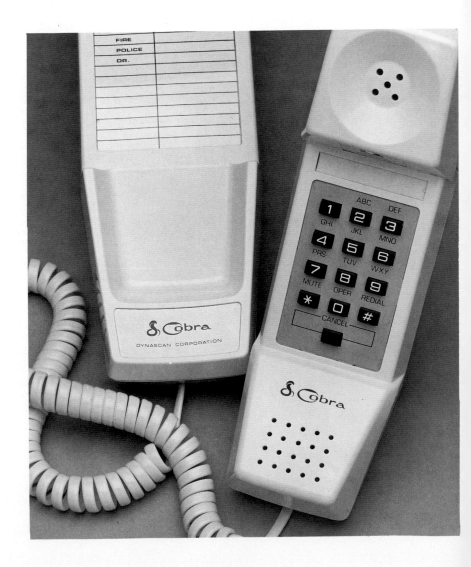

Client Eaglewood Development
Designer Ken Roscoe
Design Firm Creative Works

Client Eckerd Drug Company
Designer Larry Edlavitch
Design Firm The Berni Corporation

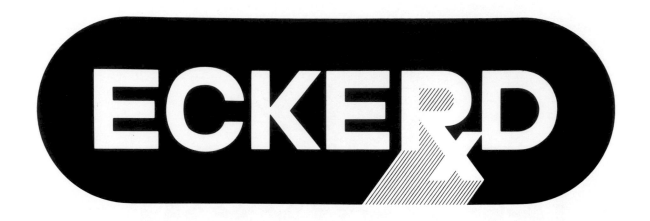

Client Elgin Sweeper Company
Designers Burt Benjamin, Judy Sloan,
Michael Maciorowski, Ted Fries
Design Firm E. Burton Benjamin Associates

Client Equis Corporation
Designers Norman Din (Art Director)
Beth Martin
Design Firm Din & Associates

Equis

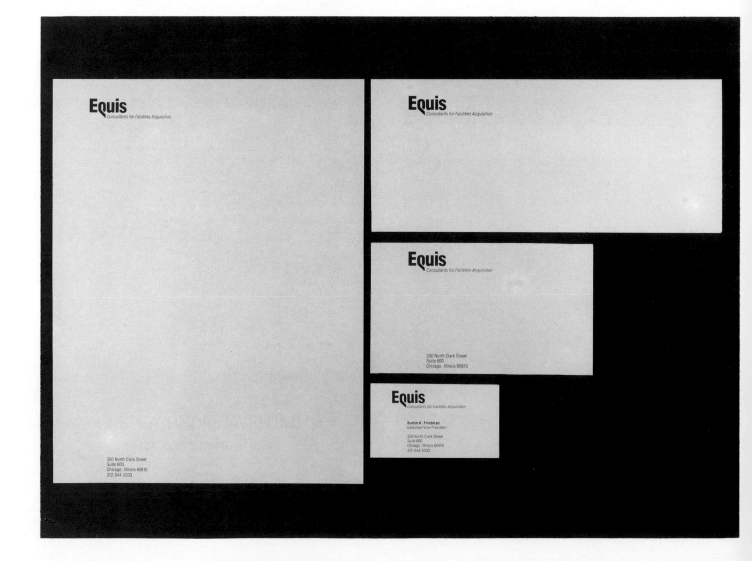

Client Farrell's Restaurant
& Ice Cream Parlour
Designer Howard York (Creative Director),
Jan Schockner
Design Firm S&O Consultants

Client Father Flanagan's Boys' Home
Designer John Morning
Design Firm John Morning Design, Inc.

Client Foundation of The Dramatist Guild
Designer Marvin Berk
Design Firm Creative Images in Inc.

write a play
Young Playwrights' Festival

Client Gateway Park Hotel
Designers Mike Dambrowski, Ted Nuttall
Design Firm Dambrowski Nuttall
　　　　　　　Design Associates

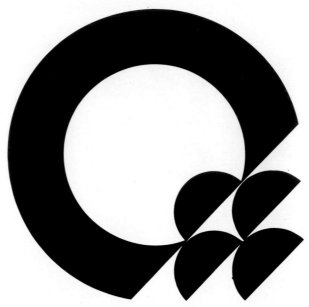

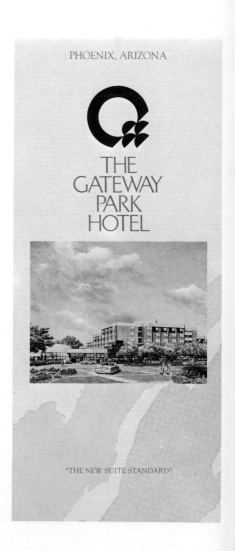

Client Genesee & Wyoming
Designer Milton Glaser
Design Firm Milton Glaser Inc.

Client Hammond Electronics, Inc.
Designer Joe Bailey
Design Firm McAllister-Barker Associates

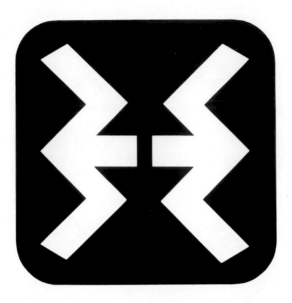

PUBLISHED BY HARCOURTS GALLERY   VOLUME II, NUMBER 1, 1981

M. H. de Young Museum

Exclusive Tiffany Exhibit

The M. H. de Young Memorial Museum, site of exhibits such as "The Splendors of Dresden" and "Treasures of Tutankhamun" which attracted the public in unprecedented numbers during recent years, has an exhibition scheduled from April 23rd through August 8th of 1981 that promises to impressively rival all previous attendance records. For the first time in the United States, more than 300 objects associated with Louis Comfort Tiffany will be on public display, the culmination of several years of work by the Fine Arts Museums of San Francisco, with the support of The Museum Society.

Funded by a grant from Shaklee Corporation, which has long evidenced its support of the City's artistic and cultural efforts through substantial contributions, the huge exhibition includes architectural details, stained glass windows, furniture, blown glass, ceramics, enamel, silver and bronze objects as well as the famous Tiffany lamps. Works have been selected from the collection of the Charles Hosmer Morse Foundation of Winter Park, Florida, as assembled by Mr. and Mrs. Hugh F. McKean.

The exhibition has been carefully planned so as to present a major, definitive examination of the diverse artistic production of Tiffany (1848-1933) and the Tiffany Studios. It will place this body of work in its historic context and demonstrate how Tiffany's personal search for order and beauty provided a unique harmony that transcended both the Arts and Crafts Movement and the Art Noveau style.

The son of the founder of Tiffany & Company, Louis C. Tiffany first studied painting, both in the United States and abroad, and by the age of thirty was one of America's best known artists. But, possibly inspired by the 12th and 13th century stained glass he had seen on his European sojourns, Tiffany turned toward the decorative arts, especially glass

making, and entered the field of interior decoration in 1879.

Tiffany supplied objects that were not generally available in 19th century America, such as exotic hangings, carvings and pottery, and designed imaginative interiors for his wealthy clients. By 1883, his fame earned him a commission to decorate the public rooms in the White House.

It was, however, the 1893 World's Columbian Exposition in Chicago that led to Tiffany's position as one of the first

A 58-inch leaded window, c. 1899, entitled "Young Woman at a Fountain," is just one of more than 300 objects comprising the upcoming Tiffany exhibition at the M. H. de Young Museum. Courtesy Doubleday & Co., "The Lost Treasures of L. C. Tiffany," by H. F. McKean, 1980.

American artists to enjoy international influence. After exhibiting his glass in a chapel he designed there, Tiffany was contacted by a Parisian art dealer who was planning a new gallery. In 1895, Le Salon de l'Art Noveau opened, and Tiffany was represented along with Toulouse Lautrec, Pierre Bonnard, Auguste Rodin, Rene Lalique and Aubrey Beardsley, among others.

By 1902, when Tiffany Studios was organized, Tiffany was responsible for a wide range of fine crafts: textiles, fabrics, rugs, hangings, embroideries and needlework, upholsteries and furniture, mosaics, leaded glass, lighting fixtures, bronzework and brasses, ornamental windows, frescoes, altar crosses, sacred vessels, vestaments, memorials in the
(continued col. 1, pg. 2)

Nineteen Eighty

The Year in Review

During 1980, Harcourts Gallery experienced some of the most exciting exhibits and events in its fifty-two year history, the result of many months and even years of preparation and planning. Harcourts began the decade of the 80's with a new symbol of corporate identity, an award winning logo representing the Gallery in all national, regional and international publications.

The corporate office and additional gallery space, consisting of 1,500 square feet, were officially opened at 550 Powell in early March, following a January showing of colorful contemporary tapestries by Mexican and American artists. This preview was followed by exhibits of drawings and paintings by Luis Filcer, and marble, steel and bronze sculptures by Andrew Fagan.

After the corporate offices had been moved across the street, the third floor of the Gallery was transformed into a sweeping length of gently faceted walls
(continued col. 1, pg. 6)

Client Health Action Press
Designer John A. Dixon
Design Firm Graphic Design Works

Client Honeybear Industries
Designer Lauren Smith
Design Firm Lauren Smith Design

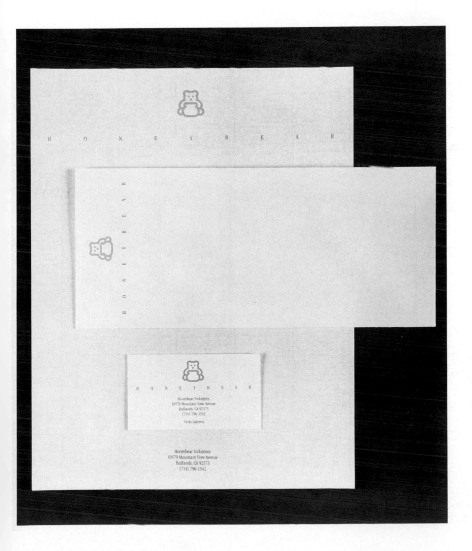

Client Houston Ad Hoc Tunnel Committee
Designers Steve Harding and Larry Roberts
Design Firm 3D/International

Client New York Dept. of Commerce
Designer Milton Glaser
Design Firm Milton Glaser Inc.

I ♥ NY®

Client Indus Systems
Designers Carlos Huerta,
David Nakashita
Design Firm Huerta Design Associates

Client International Business Phone Corp.
Designer Erwin Lefkowitz
Design Firm Erwin Lefkowitz & Associates

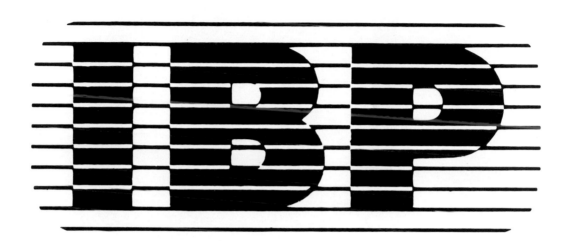

INTERNATIONAL BUSINESS PHONE CORP.

TELEPHONE SYSTEMS
PROPOSAL

Client Kathy Bruce, Copywriter
Designer Joe Bailey
Design Firm Joe Bailey: Advertising
                by Design

Client Kent County Memorial Hospital
Designer George Delany
Design Firm Delany Design Group, Inc.

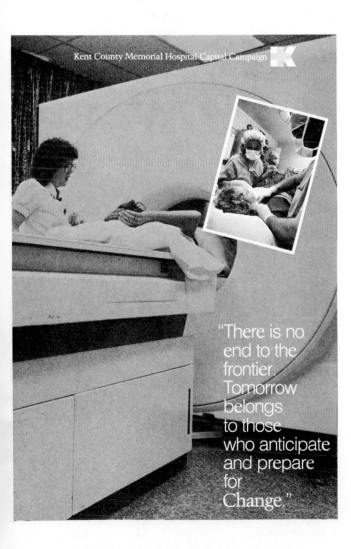

Kent County Memorial Hospital Capital Campaign

"There is no end to the frontier. Tomorrow belongs to those who anticipate and prepare for Change."

Client KETC Public Television, St. Louis
Designer Richard Deardorff
Design Firm Overlook Howe Consulting
Group

KETC

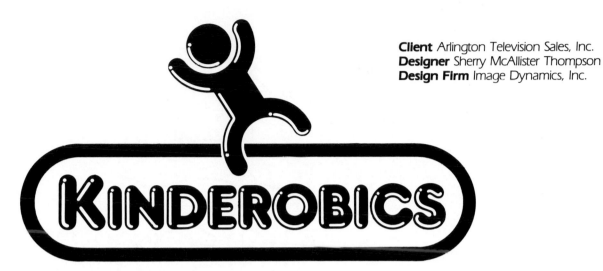

Client Arlington Television Sales, Inc.
Designer Sherry McAllister Thompson
Design Firm Image Dynamics, Inc.

Kinderobics, the television exercise program designed by a leading California pediatrician-physiologist, aims to help little bodies as they develop and grow. Sure, the kids would like to exercise, just like Mom and Dad. But doing the same exercises may not be good for those young muscles and bones. Kinderobics deals with that problem with activities designed to be best for children. Kinderobics will keep the kids glued to their sets before they try their new exercises out in the yard or down at the gym! Kinderobics comes either as a 3½-minute insert into your children's programming or as a 30-minute separate feature. Choose one or choose both! They're the latest from Arlington Television Sales!

Although they may be quickly moving along toward adulthood, pre-teens sometimes need special exercise programs too, to help their bodies get through the fastest growth spurt of their lives. Juniorobics is designed for them by the same leading California pediatrician-physiologist who originated Kinderobics for Arlington Television Sales. Also available as 3½-minute inserts or 30-minute shows, Juniorobics is perfect for the "after school" time period. Juniorobics provides the anchor you need to get that youth market and keep it. Juniorobics falls in line with the drive for good health that's sweeping the nation. And now — for the first time — there's a way for young pre-teens — the group that needs to belong — to become a part of the action!

Call Arlington Television Sales

Jeff Simmons
(301) 849-2300

Bob Oppenheim
(213) 450-6600

Client KUER FM 90, NPR Affiliate
Designer Scott Engen
Design Firm IMS Graphic Services

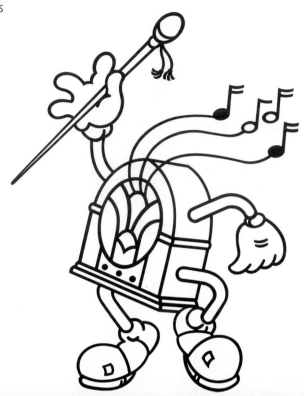

Client LA/NY
Designers Michael Waitsman,
Liane Sebastian
Design Firm Synthesis Concepts, Inc.

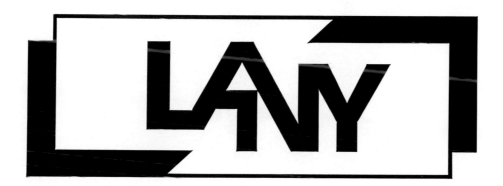

LA/NY MUSIC
9034 SUNSET BLVD., SUITE 101
LOS ANGELES, CA 90069
213/273-1667

Client Libby's
Designer Jerome Gould
Design Firm Gould & Associates, Inc.

Libby's
Libby's
Libby's

Client Link Telecommunications
Designer Stavros Cosmopulos
Design Firm Cosmopulos, Crowley & Daly

Client Lithographix
Designers Don Weller, Dan Hanrahan
Design Firm The Weller Institute for the
            Cure of Design, Inc.

Client Maine Woods
Designers Stavros Cosmopulos,
Tom Demeter
Design Firm Cosmopulos, Crowley & Daly

Client Massmeetings
Designers Stavros Cosmopulos,
Tom Demeter
Design Firm Cosmopulos, Crowley & Daly

Client McCullock Corporation
Designer Don Weller
Design Firm The Weller Institute for the
Cure of Design, Inc.

McCULLOCH
CORPORATION

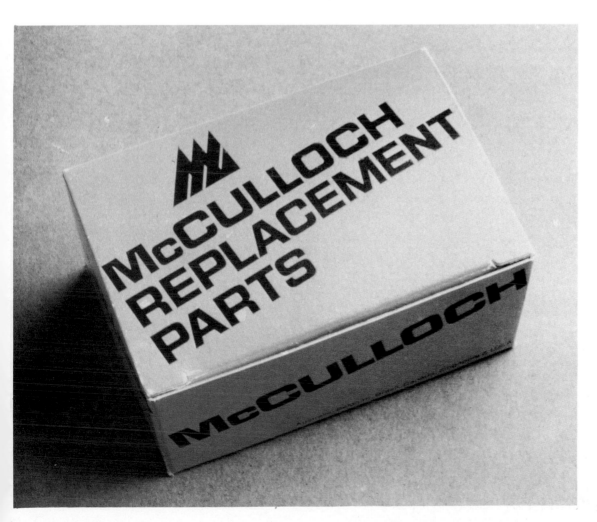

Client Meadowood
Designer Michael Cronan
Design Firm Michael Patrick
Cronan/Design Inc.

Meadowood

Meadowood Music Camp
Session I - 1981

Michael Agins/Guitar/San Anselmo
Amy Jean Archer/Flute/Berkeley
Eric L. Axelrode/Trombone/Orinda
Daniel S. Bailis/Trumpet/San Rafael
Edgar Q. Banks/Drums/San Rafael
Paul A. Beehler/Clarinet/Orinda
Stacy A. Beehler/Flute/Orinda
Cressey Belden/Clarinet/Santa Rosa
Shana M. Berger/Ballet/Berkeley
Jenny E. Berke/Violin/Oakland
Jessica L. Berman/Flute/San Francisco
Sarah Boushey/Violin/San Francisco
Leslie Brand/Flute/Berkeley
Bonnie J. Burroughs/Flute/Inverness
Suzanne A. Cantlay/Piano/Aptos
Susan D. Carter/Piano/San Francisco
Sarah H. Cave/Flute/Berkeley
John M. Chachere/Clarinet/Berkeley
Marlis Corning/Violin/Mill Valley
Elyse Costy/Ballet/Hayward
Daniel J. Cotton/Clarinet/Oakland
Holden Daniels/Alto Sax/San Rafael
Amy C. Davis/Flute/Etna
Donald I. Davis/Guitar/Oakland
Joanna F. Davis/Flute/Calistoga
Sunee DeBolt/Piano/Piedmont
Michael DeCola/French Horn/Berkeley
Lorae B. Donelson/Cello/Berkeley
Jacob S. Edelstein/Alto Sax/Berkeley
Sarah K. Edelstein/Cello/Berkeley
Jennifer Eden/Flute/Berkeley
Rebecca S. Einwohner/Violin/Berkeley
Kate A. Foley/Flute/Berkeley
Lisa M. Gee/Piano/San Francisco

Brad D. Golditch/Tenor Sax/San Rafael
James S. Goody/Clarinet/Piedmont
Jeremy S. Goody/Trumpet/Piedmont
Daniel M. Greif/Saxophone/Berkeley
Jason P. Gruen/French Horn/Berkeley
Anne E. Haberkern/Violin/Berkeley
Samantha Haimovitch/Flute/Berkeley
Heather Hamm/Flute/Petaluma
Angela P. Hayes/Violin/Mendocino
Xochil M. Hensley/Piano/San Rafael
Douglas P. Hiatt/Trumpet/Malibu
Joshua D. Hoffert/Guitar/Windsor
Nicole J. Howard/Flute/Mill Valley
Megan N. Inaba/Violin/Berkeley
Kimi Jacobson/Violin/San Anselmo
W. Gavin Jensen/Saxophone/Vacaville
Davin L. Jendrich/Violin/Mill Valley
Eleonore M. Johnson/Flute/Berkeley
Thomas C. Johnson/Trumpet/Berkeley
Ling-Yen Jones/Dance/Berkeley
Jamien Jordan/Flute/Berkeley
Viral V. Joshi/Violin/Oakland
Tracy Kanbara/Flute/Corte Madera
Jason Kaneko/Trumpet/Berkeley
Linda K. Kaplan/Ballet/Berkeley
Stephanie D. Kirby/Clarinet/San Rafael
Jochua C. Klausner/Coronet/Berkeley
Lee S. Kuerbis/Cello/Lafayette
Stepaan C. Larsen/Trumpet/Berkeley
Jennifer S. Leech/Violin/Berkeley
Fia B. Lehmann/Clarinet/Berkeley
Robert A. Lehmann/Violin/Novato
Stephen E. Lew/Oboe/Sebastopol
Rebecca Lewis/Dance/Berkeley
Brendan Liston/Trumpet/San Rafael
Erika C. Lloyd/Flute/Benicia
Jerrell Loggins/Guitar/Oakland
Gillian H. Martin/Violin/Mill Valley
Gregory McLean/Clarinet/Berkeley
Elena R. McCoy/Clarinet/Novato
Heather L. McPhail/Piano/San Rafael
Sara E. Mechanic/Violin/Oakland
Ian Meng/Cello/Walnut Creek
Melina Miyoshi/Violin/Berkeley
Owen Miyoshi/Trumpet/Berkeley
Anne Marie Modro/Flute/Sunnyvale
Harriet B. Muir/Cello/Berkeley
Aaron F. Murphy/Piano/Mill Valley
Patrick M. Murphy/Violin/Mill Valley
Andrea Nencioni/Piano/Torino, Italy
Gregory E. Noble/Clarinet/Novato
Maureen O'Brien/Clarinet/Novato
Luke C. O'Bryne/Trumpet/San Anselmo
Tatia M. Oden/Flute/Oakland
Monika Y. Olson/Piano/Berkeley
Allison Packard/Violin/Berkeley
Steven Packard/Flute/Berkeley
Maureen M. Palmer/Flute/Hamilton Base

Shelly P. Price/Alto Sax/San Jose
Shauna J. Reiff/Piano/Berkeley
Jennifer A. Rhode/Dance/Berkeley
Laura A. Ribbel/Trumpet/Novato
Laura Robinson/Pinao/Berkeley
Anthony Rojas/Flute/San Jose
Danielle S. Roland/Cello/Berkeley
Heidi M. Ronfeldt/Violin/Berkeley
Mariana J. Root/Flute/Santa Rosa
Claire C. Sallee/Violin/Davis
Kristin P. Sallee/Cello/Davis
Aleja Sanchez/Violin/Kensington
Laurie A. San Martin/Clarinet/Berkeley
Julie A. Saxe/Flute/Corte Madera
Emil Schissel/Cello/Berkeley
Adam J. Schneider/Trumpet/San Rafael
Cheryl E. Self/Violin/Berkeley
Briana H. Smolowe/Guitar/Forest Knolls
Matt S. St. John/Saxophone/Berkeley
Nicholas H. St. John/Clarinet/Berkeley
Scott F. Tallarida/Trombone/Novato
Nina A. Taschian/Viola/Berkeley
David W. Tollen/Saxophone/San Rafael
Laura A. Tollen/Flute/San Rafael
Robert-Gordon Tribble/Drums/Petaluma
Naomi A. Trier/Piano/Belmont
Elena E. Valencia/Flute/San Francisco
James Vlahos/Violin/Kensington
Andrea Wagner/Piano/Berkeley
Jason H. Walker/Trombone/Lucas Valley
Abigail O. Washburn/Piano/Mill Valley
David C. Watts/Trumpet/San Francisco
Jason Weitman/Trumpet/Malibu
Robert C. Wellington/Flute/Berkeley
Dean A. Whitbeck/Guitar/San Rafael
John R. White/Percussion/Mill Valley
Howard S. Wilner/Drums/San Rafael
James L. Wilson/Trumpet/San Francisco
Michael Wilson/Violin/Berkeley
Wendy Wilson/Cello/Oakland
Lisa S. Wishovich/Clarinet/San Rafael
Darren Wong/Violin/Daly City
Jeremy Workman/Trumpet/Berkeley
Brian J. Wright/Alto Sax/San Rafael
Ondine T. Young/Violin/Berkeley

THE PLAYERS

SUMMER 1981

M

Client Men
Designer Stavros Cosmopulos
Design Firm Cosmopulos, Crowley & Daly

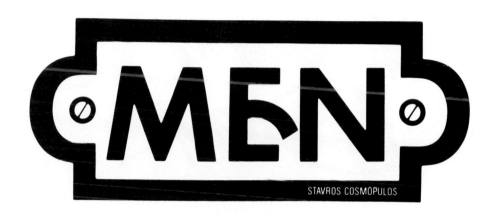

STAVROS COSMOPULOS

Client Mireille Dansereau
Designer Vahe Fattal
Design Firm Fattal & Collins

Un film de Mireille Dansereau

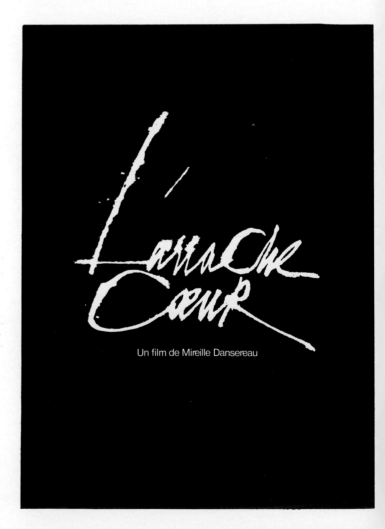

Client Montair
Designers Greg Beck, Anthony Sini
Design Firm Sandage Advertising
& Marketing

Montair

Client Municipal Savings and Loan
Designer Frederick A. Kail
Design Firm Telesis

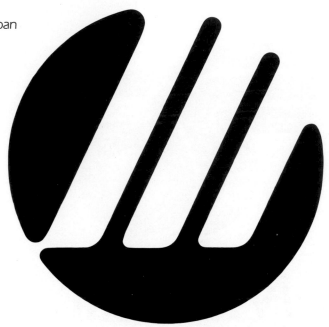

Client National Polymer
Designer Norman Din (Art Director)
Design Firm Din & Associates

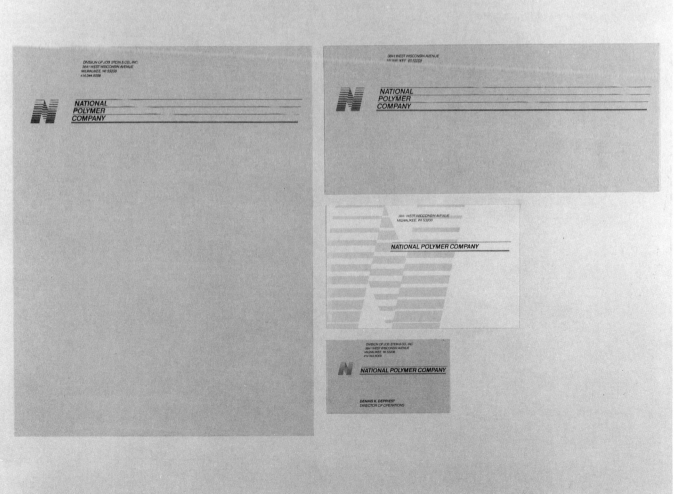

Client Nebraska Savings
Designers Howard York (Creative Director)
Fran Koenig (Design Director)
Design Firm S&O Consultants

Nebraska Savings™

Client Nelson & Bauman
Designer Vahe Fattal
Design Firm Fattal & Collins

Client New Penn Press
Designers Amy Blake and Robert Barancik
Design Firm Blake + Barancik Design Group

Client NY City Special Olympics
Designer Marco DePlano
Design Firm Marco DePlano & Associates

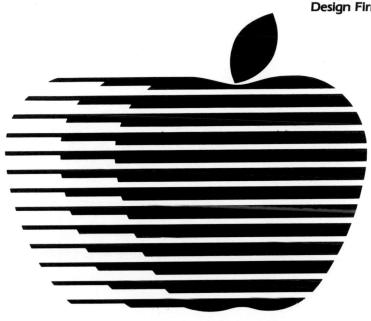

Client New York Rail Car
Designer Johannes Regn
Design Firm Regn/Califano

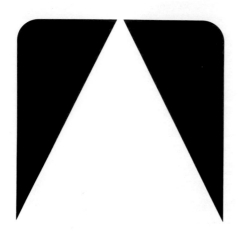

New York Rail Car

Client Norwest Bancorp
Designers Howard York (Creative Director),
Fran Koenig (Design Director)
Design Firm S&O Consultants

NORWEST BANKS

Client Overlook Press
Designer Milton Glaser
Design Firm Milton Glaser Inc.

TVSK

Client Amoco Oil Company
Designer Larry Forgard
Design Firm Standard Oil (in-house)

★ ★ ★ ★ ★ ★ ★ ★ ★ ★ ★

**Public
Affairs
Communication
Effort**

**A program for dealers and jobbers in Amoco
Oil Company's Western Marketing Region.**

Client Panama Marine Ltd., Subsidiary of
The Aleut Corporation, Alaska
Designer Mike Fieldhouse
Design Firm Mike Fieldhouse,
Graphic Design

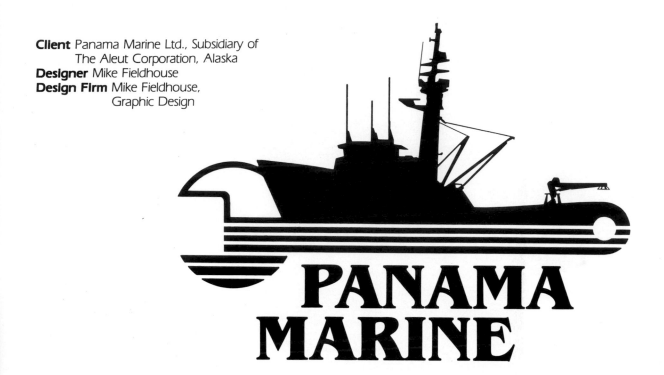

PANAMA MARINE

Client Panda Inn
Designers John Follis, Connie Beck
Design Firm Follis Design

© 1982 Panda Inn

PANDA INN
MANDARIN CUISINE

聚豐園

Client Partners of The Americas
Designer Malcolm Grear Designers, Inc.
Design Firm Malcolm Grear Designers, Inc.

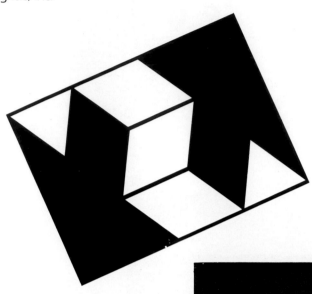

Client Paul Faulise Music Inc.
Designer Michael Lafortezza
Design Firm Lam Design Associates, Inc.

The F&D Double Valve Bass Trombone

Daily Warm-up and Maintenance Exercises by Paul Faulise

PF Music Co.

Client Plasmafusion, Inc.
Designer Janice Weisler
Design Firm JTW Graphic Design

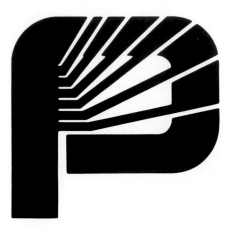

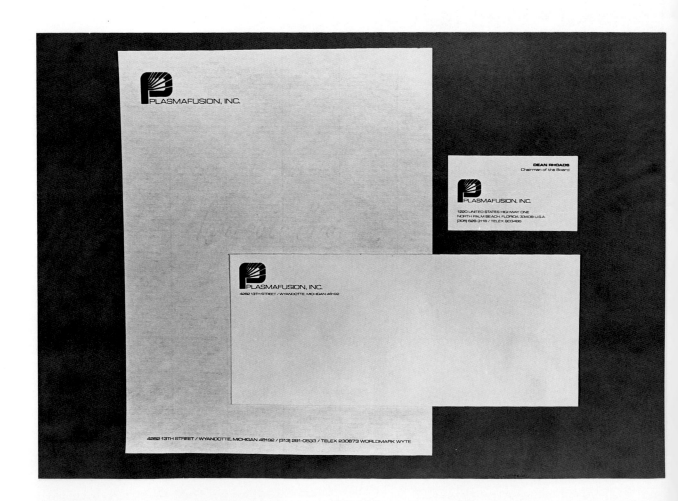

Client Polyfibers
Designers Don Weller,
Chikako Matsubayashi
Design Firm The Weller Institute for the
Cure of Design, Inc.

Client Quackers
Designers Jack Anderson, Ellen Wenrich
Design Firm John Hornall Design Works

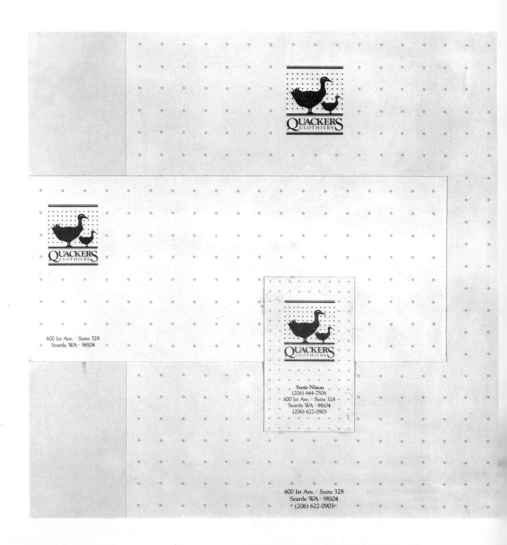

Client Reliance Pen & Pencil
Designer Ron Bradford
Design Firm Bradford-Cout Design

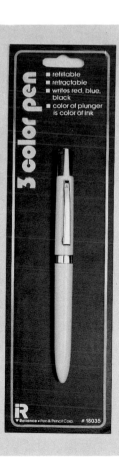

Client Richard Sachs Cycles, Craftsman
Builder of Lightweight Bicycle Frames
Designer Danielle Dimston
Design Firm Danielle Dimston

Client Robert M. Eginton, Photographer
Designer Joe Bailey
Design Firm Joe Bailey: Advertising
by Design

Client San Antonio International Airport
Designer Cheri Groom
Design Firm Atkins & Associates
Advertising, Inc.

Client Santa Barbara County Foodbank
Designer James Palam
Design Firm Palam Design

Client San Francisco Symphony
Designer Michael Cronan
Design Firm Michael Patrick
Cronan/Design Inc.

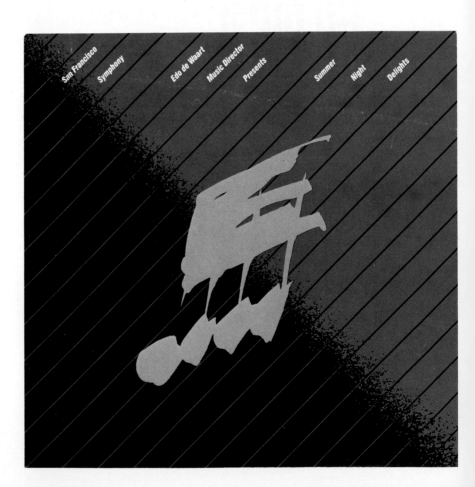

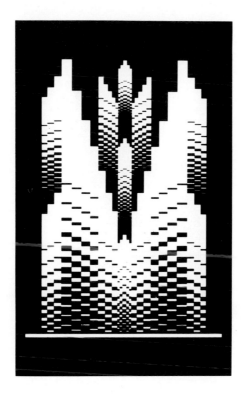

Client San Francisco Symphony
Designer Michael Cronan
Design Firm Michael Patrick
Cronan/Design Inc.

*T*he "king of instruments" is waiting, the pipes are tuned, and the premiere season is about to begin. There's an extraordinary extravaganza at midnight, recitals featuring internationally renowned organists, and a truly spectacular non-stop marathon with the San Francisco Symphony. Experience the sound of its 7,700 pipes. Celebrate with us.

Sunday, May 20
8:30 p.m.

Bay Area Organists Recital

Eileen Coggin	Richard Purvis
Ralph Hooper	Susan Summerfield
Edwin Flath	David Babbitt
Robert Newton	Pamela Decker
Herbert Nanney	Richard Bradshaw
Eric Stevens	Robert Walker
Richard Webb	Fred Tulan

Distinguished Bay Area organists join together in a grand celebration of the Ruffatti and Noack organs in a widely varied program including works by Bach, Couperin, Barber, and Liszt.

All programs are at Davies Symphony Hall
All programs subject to change.

Wednesday, June 27
7:00 p.m.

A Marathon Salute

Neeme Järvi, conductor
San Francisco Symphony

Organists:	
	Gillian Weir
David Fuller	Fred Tulan
John Weaver	Leonard Raver
David Schrader	John Rose
Marilyn Mason	Philip Brunelle

Your opportunity to hear the San Francisco Symphony and renowned organists perform in a three-hour marathon salute to the organ including solo masterpieces and bravura concertos. Jongen's "Symphonie concertante" and the Dupré Symphony for Organ and Orchestra are included in the program.

Client San Francisco Symphony
Designer Michael Cronan
Design Firm Michael Patrick
Cronan/Design Inc.

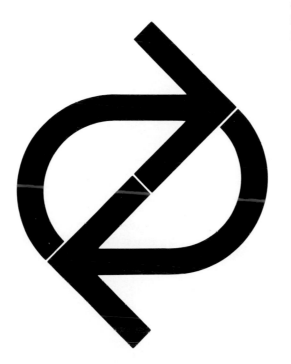

Client The Short Line Bus, Inc.
Designer Malcolm Grear Designers, Inc.
Design Firm Malcolm Grear Designers, Inc.

Client Snoopy's Ice Cream and Cookie Co.
Designers Primo Angeli, Charles Schultz,
        Mark Jones
Design Firm Primo Angeli Graphics

Client Southern California Edison Co.
Designer Jerome Gould
Design Firm Gould & Associates, Inc.

Client Southern California Gas Co.
Designer Jerome Gould
Design Firm Gould & Associates, Inc.

Client H.P. Hood, Inc.-Boston Mass.
Designer John Digianni (Creative Director)
Design Firm Gianninoto Associates

STRASSEL'S ™

Client Syntex Corporation
Designers Lance Wyman, Bill Cannan
Design Firm Wyman & Cannan Co., Ltd.

THE DEVELOPMENT OF THE NEW SYNTEX SYMBOL

The letter "S" from the Syntex name was the starting point for the design of the new Syntex Symbol.

The sea represents the beginnings of life, and a wave shape also suggests the "S" form which was adapted to the Symbol.

A globe – the earth as seen from space – symbolizes the international involvement of Syntex in the life sciences.

The new Syntex Symbol is, thus, more than a stylized "S". It is a synthesis of images meaningful to Syntex, a symbol adaptable for use in many combinations and configurations; a strong symbol that can serve us well.

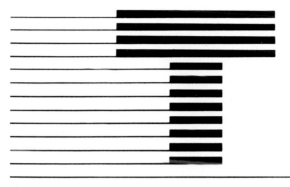

Client Tartan Laboratories Incorporated
Designer Ronnie Savion
Design Firm The Graphic Suite

TARTAN

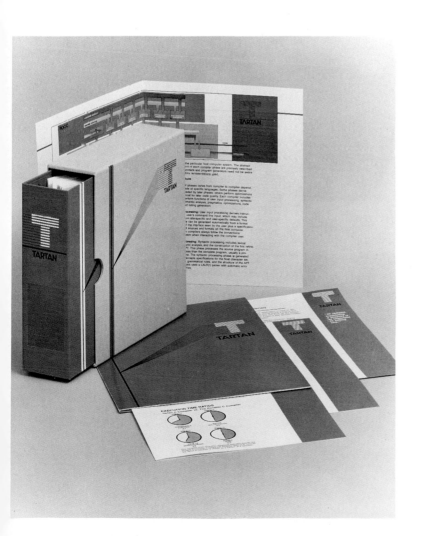

Client Tektra, Inc.
Designer Randy Hull
Design Firm Randall Hull Design Office

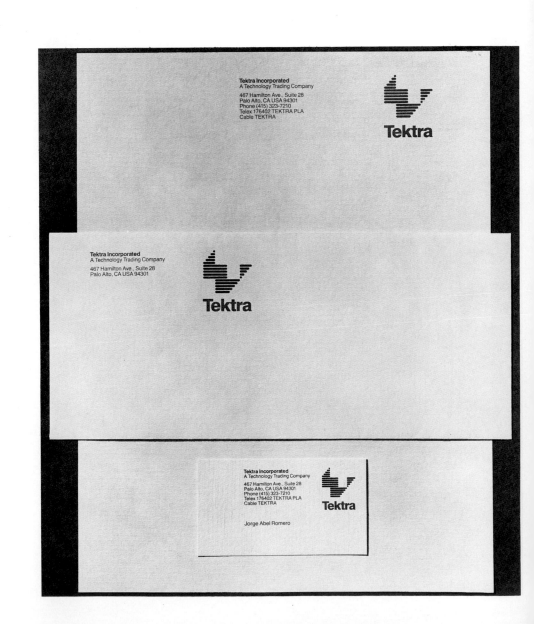

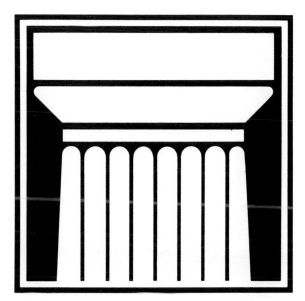

Client The Athenian School
Designer Ron Shore
Design Firm Shore Design

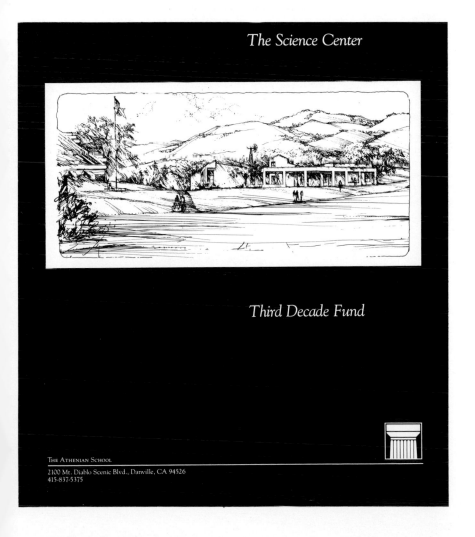

Client The Cleanup Crew
Designer Lauren Smith
Design Firm Lauren Smith Design

THE BRUSH OFF

We're the Cleanup Crew and we'd like to make your building shine! We're a property maintenance service with nearly 20 years of janitorial experience. But here's the best part: We think we can save you both time and money! Because the Cleanup Crew offers an unusually wide range of services, one call to us can usually take care of all your cleaning problems. Since there's no need to bring in several contractors, your apartment or office can often be ready for the next tenant within 24 hours! And your satisfaction is always guaranteed.

805-489-9730
805-481-4370

THE FOOT DOCTOR

Client The Foot Doctor
Designers Randy Hull, Erin Smith
Design Firm Randall Hull Design Office

Client The Lacrosse Foundation
Designer Frederick A. Kail
Design Firm Telesis

Client The Mannes Circle
Designer Marvin Berk
Design Firm Creative Images in Inc.

THE MANNES CIRCLE
to enjoy music and encourage its performance

Client The Prudential Insurance Company
Designer Lee & Young Communications
Design Firm Lee & Young Communications

The **Prudential**

Insurance &
Financial Services

Client The Tarquini Organization,
Architectural Firm
Designer Richard Yeager
Design Firm Richard Yeager Associates, Inc.

The Tarquini Organization ... architects and planners with a
capacity and commitment to meet new challenges based on
long-held standards of excellence and a continuing record of
accomplishment. With firm roots in the highest quality design
that stretch back to 1947, The Tarquini Organization has shown
steady growth via its capacity to manage total planning—
programming — design — construction tasks for projects of
varying size and scope. Its mark remains on the landscape in
the form of enduring design that is, at once, functional and
pleasing; yet, on time and within budget. As we continue our
growth (you may have known us as Tarquini, Liszewski Plus,
in the past), our design professionals will continue to apply
problem solving skills—and the
insight born of decades of
experience — to your
needs, while emphasiz-
ing imaginative and
flexible planning
to meet the
challenges
of the
80's.

A professional association of architects and planners. 1812 Federal Street, Camden, NJ 08105. 609/365-7270.

Client The Zebra Zucchini
Designer Stavros Cosmopulos
Design Firm Cosmopulos, Crowley & Daly

Client UCLA Extension
Designer Vahe Fattal
Design Firm Fattal & Collins

The Arts · UCLA Extension

The Arts · UCLA Extension · Fall Quarter 1981

Client UCLA Extension/Dentistry
Designer Vahe Fattal
Design Firm Fattal & Collins

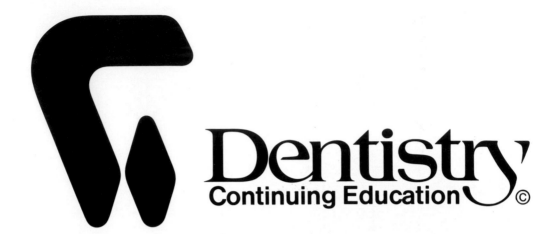

UCLA Extension

Fall 1982 - Winter 1983

Client Universal Printing
Designer Bill McDermott
Design Firm McDermott Design

Client U.S. Navy (Exchanges/Worldwide)
Designer Donald E. Gove
Design Firm Visual Research & Design

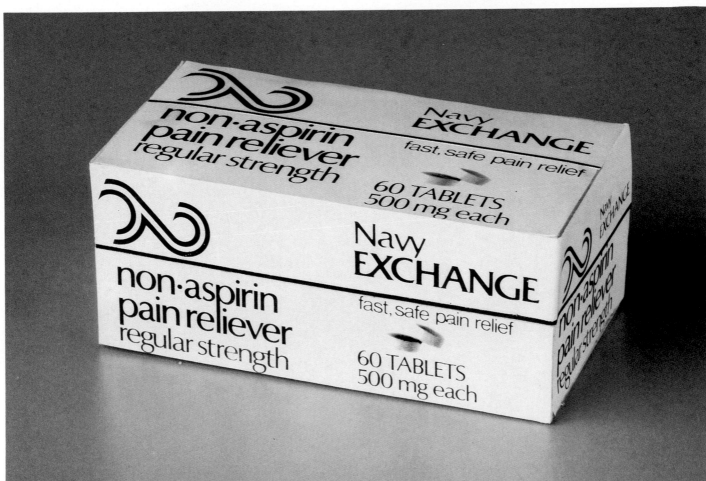

Client Valleylab, Inc.
Designer Robert W. Taylor
Design Firm Robert W. Taylor Design, Inc.

Client Verlaine, Inc.
Designers George Delany,
Catherine McGuinness
Design Firm Delany Design Group, Inc.

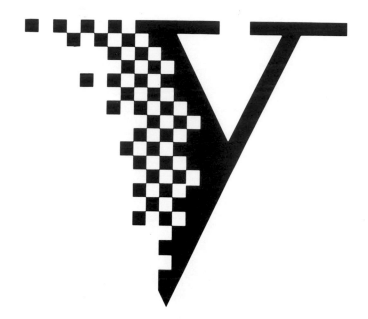

Client Walt Disney Productions
Designer Special Projects Group
Design Firm Landor Associates

Disney

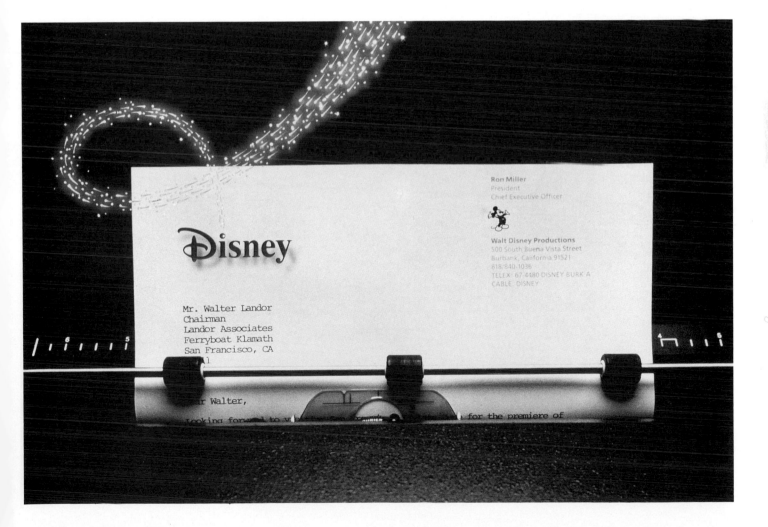

Client Washington D.C. Convention Center
Designer Lance Wyman
Design Firm Lance Wyman Ltd.

WEST BEACH

Client West Beach, Indiana Dunes
Designers Gary Brown and Ralph Lazar
Design Firm Herbst, Lazar, Rogers & Bell Inc.

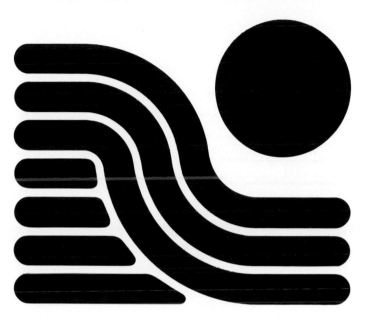

Client West Suburban Hospital Medical
Center, Immediate Care Center
Designer Richard Wittosch
Design Firm Contours Consulting
Design Group

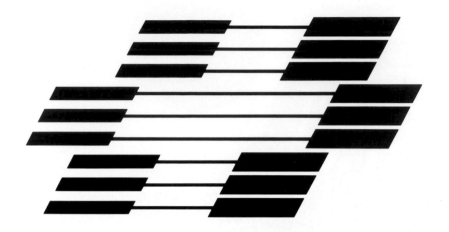

Client Wilson Foods Corporation
Designer Richard Deardorff
Design Firm Overlook Howe Consulting
Group

Client World Wide Security, Inc.
Designer Constance Kovar
Design Firm Constance Kovar
          Graphic Design, Inc.

Client Wyndham Management Company,
Cable Beach
Designers Steve Harding, Bobbi Long
Design Firm 3D/International

Client YMCA Project Safe Place
Designer Tony Beard
Design Firm Design Works, Inc.

Client Adventure Films
Designer Jack Anderson
Design Firm John Hornall Design Works

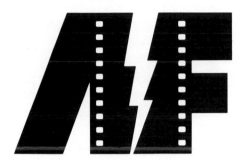

Client Affiliate Artists
Designer Michael Aron
Design Firm Pushpin Lubalin Peckolick

Client Akron General Medical Center
Designers Jeff Sturm, Carol Wetshtein
Design Firm Jef Sturm Graphic Design

Client Applied Decision Technology
Designer Steven B. Rousso
Design Firm Rousso + Wagner

Client Arizona Multihousing Association
Designers Mike Dambrowski, Ted Nuttall
Design Firm Dambrowski Nuttall
Design Associates

Client Arnold/Oroweat Food Corp.
Designer C.M. Seminario
Design Firm The Berni Corporation

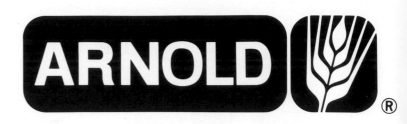

Client Asay & Associates
Designers Michael Smith, Carole Nervig
Design Firm Carole Nervig/Graphic Design

Client Atlantic Cable Television
Publishing Corporation
Designer Constance Kovar
Design Firm Constance Kovar Graphic
Design Inc.

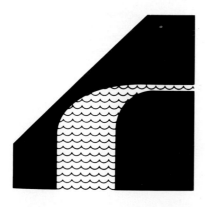

ASAY & ASSOCIATES

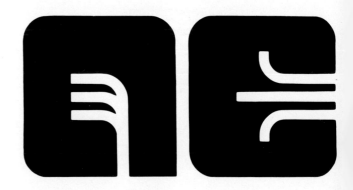

Client Aviall, Inc.
Designers Jeffrey D. Lawson
            Dan Hanrahan
Design Firm Dennis S. Juett & Associates Inc.

Client Backsavers, Inc.
Designer Susie Brandt
Design Firm Brandt Designs

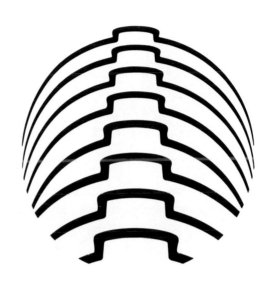

Client Bechet's (Jazz Cafe)
Designer D. Bruce Zahor
Design Firm Zahor Design Incorporated

Client Bergelectric
Designer Don Weller
Design Firm The Weller Institute for the
            Cure of Design, Inc.

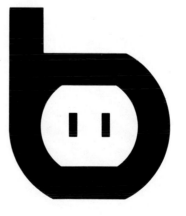

Client Biodyne Industries
Designer Jeffrey D. Lawson
Design Firm Dennis S. Juett & Associates Inc.

Client Blue Chip Office Automation Inc.
Designer Jim Hilborn
Design Firm Herbst, Lazar, Rogers & Bell Inc.

BIODYNE

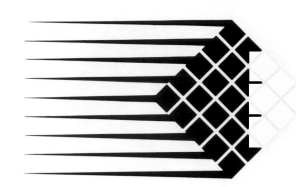

Client Bridgeport Hospital,
Cardiac Rehabilitation Unit
Designer Danielle Dimston
Design Firm Armstrong Design
Consultants

Client Brownlee Jewelers
Designer Steven B. Rousso
Design Firm Rousso + Wagner

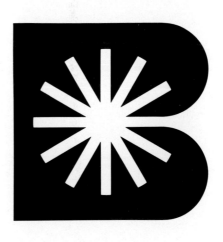

Client Cashin Systems
Designer Clint Morgan
Design Firm John Waters Associates, Inc.

CA$HIN

Client Cat Clinic
Designers Jack Anderson, Cliff Chung
Design Firm John Hornall Design Works

Client CBS Video
Designer Alan Peckolick
Design Firm Lubalin Peckolick Associates

Client Charles Lee, Chiropractor
Designer Tim Hartung
Design Firm Hartung & Associates, Ltd.

Client Cherri Oakley Co.-Nakamoto
Designer Don Arday
Design Firm Eisenberg, Inc.

NAKAMOTO

Client Chicago Bank of Commerce
Designer George Kubricht
Design Firm Comcorp, Inc.

Client Chicago Crane & Machinery Co.
Designer Gary R. Olson
Design Firm The Olson Group

Chicago Crane Company

Client Ckat & Associates
Designer Constance Kovar
Design Firm Constance Kovar
             Graphic Design, Inc.

Client Commerce Bank
Designer Richard Yeager
Design Firm Richard Yeager Associates, Inc.

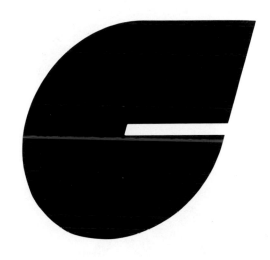

Client Command Travel Inc.
Designer D. Bruce Zahor
Design Firm Zahor Design Incorporated

Client Colorado Electric
Designers Michael Smith, Carole Nervig
Design Firm Carole Nervig/Graphic Design

COLORADO ELECTRIC

Client Condor Automotive
Designer Don Connelly
Design Firm Don Connelly & Associates

Client Cresent Industries
Designer Bob Mynster
Design Firm Studiographix

Client Dallas Ballet
Designers Scott T. Ray
Don Grimes (Calligrapher)
Design Firm Eisenberg, Inc.

Client Digital Controls Inc.
Designer Steven B. Rousso
Design Firm Garrett/Lewis/Johnson

Client Docutel-Olivetti
Designer John March
Design Firm Eisenberg, Inc.

Client Evans Withycombe Inc.
Designer Chris Yaranoff
Design Firm Slesinger, Yaranoff & Associates

Client Garrett Sound
Designers Michael Waitsman,
Liane Sebastian
Design Firm Synthesis Concepts, Inc

Client Goethe House New York
Designer Marvin Berk
Design Firm Creative Images in Inc.

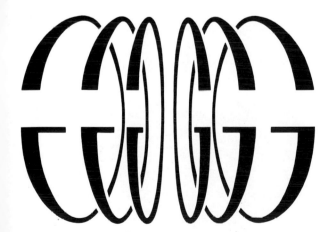

Client Independence Bank
Designer Richard Yeager
Design Firm Richard Yeager Associates, Inc.

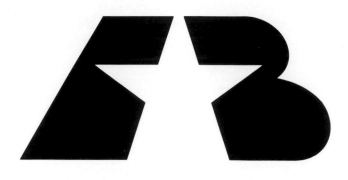

Client International Women's Writing Guild
Designer D. Bruce Zahor
Design Firm Zahor Design Incorporated

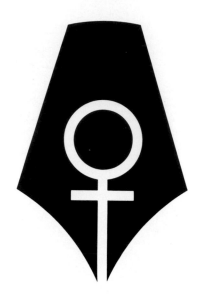

Client Interstate Building Corporation
Designer C.M. Seminario
Design Firm The Berni Corporation

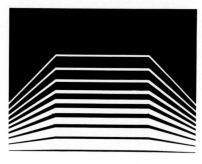 INTERSTATE
BUILDING
CORPORATION

Client K.E. Peterson & Associates
(Guest Relations Consultant)
Designer Kym Abrams
Design Firm Sturm Communications
Group, Inc.

Client Lance S.A.; Mexico City
Designer Richard Deardorff
Design Firm Overlook Howe Consulting
Group

Client Lee Liberman Corporate and
Marketing Communications
Designers Louis Nelson, Peter Scavuzzo
Design Firm Louis Nelson Associates Inc.

Client Legume, Inc.
Designer Paul D. Miller
Design Firm Paul D. Miller Enterprises Inc.

Client Matthews Custom Boots
Designer Steven Levine
Design Firm Creative Images in Inc.

Client Michael Sands Construction Co.
Designer Tim Hartung
Design Firm Hartung & Associates, Ltd.

Client Mount Holyoke College
Designer Malcolm Grear Designers, Inc.
Design Firm Malcolm Grear Designers, Inc.

Client Mutual of New York
Designers Clint Morgan, John Waters
Design Firm John Waters Associates, Inc.

Client National Engineering
Design Firm Babcock & Schmid

Client Neptco
Designer Malcolm Grear Designers, Inc.
Design Firm Malcolm Grear Designers, Inc.

Client Pepsi Cola
Designer Jerome Gould
Design Firm Gould & Associates, Inc.

Client Personal Financial Progress
Designer Don Weller
Design Firm The Weller Institute for the
Cure of Design, Inc.

Client Peter Kaplan Photography
Designer Alan Peckolick
Design Firm Lubalin Peckolick Associates

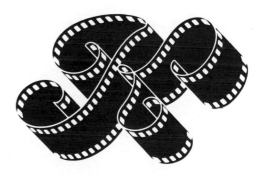

Client Pick Pro
Designer Bob Mynster
Design Firm Studiographix

Client Pindler & Pindler (Fabrics)
Designer Brian Kaneko
Design Firm Kaneko, Metzgar,
Ashcraft Design

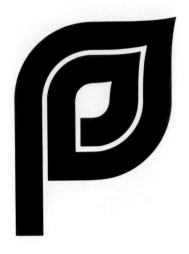

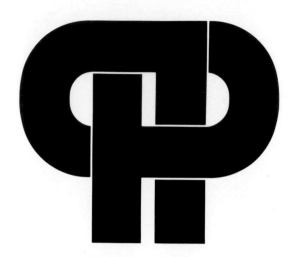

Client Pitney Bowes, Inc.
Designer Robert A. Gale
Design Firm Robert A. Gale, Inc.

Client Professional Association Management
Designer Don Connelly
Design Firm Don Connelly & Associates

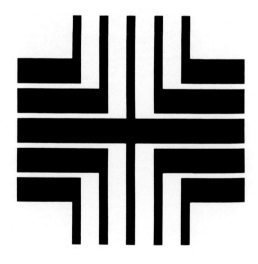

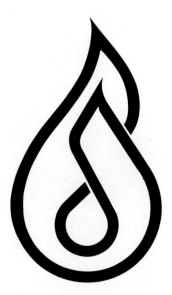

Client Quikfence,
Designer Don Weller
Design Firm The Weller Institute for the
Cure of Design, Inc.

Client Rivers Food Corporation
Designer Arthur Celedonia
Design Firm Celedonia Design

QUIKFENCE

Client Rocky Mountain Productions Inc.
Designers Louis Nelson, Dawn O'Keefe
Design Firm Louis Nelson Associates Inc.

Client Rooney, Pace Inc.
Designer Dagfinn Olsen
Design Firm Bob Glassman Design
Associates, Inc.

Client Save the Children Foundation
Designer Arthur Celedonia
Design Firm Celedonia Design

Client Schroeder's Nursery
Designer Doug Armstrong
Design Firm Comcorp, Inc.

 Save the Children

Client Sea Colony (Residential Community)
Designer Daniel Ashcraft
Design Firm Kaneko, Metzgar,
Ashcraft Design

Client Sentry Hardware Corp.
Design Firm Babcock & Schmid
Associates, Inc.

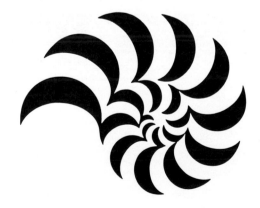

Client Silver Investment Group of
North America
Designer Berdie Stein
Design Firm Burson Marsteller

Client Simulnet
Designer Steve Ditko
Design Firm SHR Communications,
Planning & Design

Client Singer & Company
Designer Marco DePlano
Design Firm Marco DePlano & Associates

Client Skylight Inn
Design Firm Babcock & Schmid
Associates, Inc.

Client Slaughter Publishing
Designer John March
Design Firm Eisenberg, Inc.

Client Sunbelt Holdings Inc.
Designers Mike Dambrowski, Ted Nuttall
Design Firm Dambrowski Nuttall
Design Associates

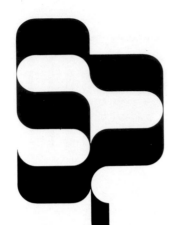

Client The Aid Station
(Immediate Medical Treatment)
Designer Kym Abrams
Design Firm Sturm Communications
Group, Inc.

Client The Acquis Group
Designer Scott T. Ray
Design Firm Eisenberg, Inc.

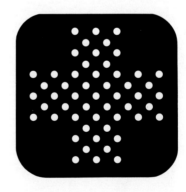

Client The Berni Corporation
Designer C.M. Seminario
Design Firm The Berni Corporation

THE BERNI
CORPORATION

Client The National Neurofibromatosis
Foundation (Elephant Man Disease)
Designer Robin Plaskoff
Design Firm Burson Marsteller Creative
Services

Client The Selin Company
Designer Don Connelly
Design Firm Don Connelly & Associates

Client The Space Coalition
Designer Robert A. Gale
Design Firm Robert A. Gale, Inc.

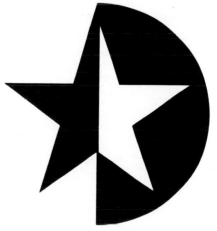

Client The Woods Group
Designer Dagfinn Olsen
Design Firm Bob Glassman Design
Associates, Inc.

Client Timothy Vermillion
Designer Mark Drury
Design Firm Eisenberg, Inc.

Client Unilogic
Designer Ronnie Savion
Design Firm The Graphic Suite

Client Valley Animal Hospital
Designers Chris Taylor, Jeff Sturm
Design Firm Jef Sturm Graphic Design

VALLEY ANIMAL HOSPITAL

Client Vaughan Walls
Designer Dennis S. Juett
Design Firm Dennis S. Juett

Client Vortran Medical Technology Inc.
Designer Thomas Collins
Design Firm Kaneko, Metzgar,
Ashcraft Design

Vaughan Walls

Client Warner Communications
Designer Alan Peckolick
Design Firm Lubalin Peckolick Associates

Client Westlake Moving & Storage System
Designer Dennis S. Juett
Design Firm Dennis S. Juett

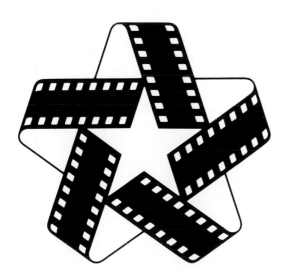

Client Wingtip Couriers
Designer Philip Waugh
Design Firm Eisenberg, Inc.

Client World Team Tennis
Designer Daniel Bernstein
Design Firm The Bernstein Design
Group, Inc.

Designers

Abbott Laboratories
14th St. and Sheridan Road
North Chicago, IL 60064

Kym Abrams Design
625 N. Michigan Ave., #1500
Chicago, IL 60611

Advertising by Design
P.O. Box 3411
Orlando, FL 32802

American Heart Association
7320 Greenville Ave.
Dallas, TX 75231

American Express Co.
125 Broad St.
New York, NY 10004

Primo Angeli Graphics
508 4th St.
San Francisco, CA 94107

Atkins & Associates, Inc.
3689 Ira Road
Bath, OH 44210

Atlantic Richfield Co.
515 S. Flower St., #1668
Los Angeles, CA 90071

Babcock & Schmid Associates, Inc.
3689 Ira Road
Bath, OH 44210

E. Burton Benjamin
3391 Summit Ave.
Highland Park, IL 60035

The Berni Corporation
666 Steamboat Road
Greenwich, CT 06830

The Bernstein Design Group, Inc.
500 N. Dearborn, #918
Chicago, IL 60610

Blake + Barancik Design Group
1919 Panama St.
Philadelphia, PA 19103

Brandt Designs
205 Kaikuono Place
Honolulu, Hawaii 96816

Brookfield Zoo
3300 Golf Road
Brookfield, IL 60153

Celedonia Design
150 E. 35th St.
New York, NY 10016

City of St. Petersburg
P.O. Box 2842
St. Petersburg, FL 33731

Comcorp, Inc.
175 N. Franklin, #203
Chicago, IL 60606

Compton Advertising
625 Madison Ave.
New York, NY 10022

Don Connelly & Associates
31 Avondale Plaza
Avondale Estates, GA 30002

Contours Consulting Design
864 Stearns Road
Bartlett, IL 60103

Cosmopolos, Crowley & Daly
250 Boylston St.
Boston, MA 02116

Creative Images in Inc.
21 W. 58th St.
New York, NY 10019

Creative Works
300 E. Prosperity Farms Road
N. Palm Beach, FL 33408

Michael Patrick Cronan/Design
1 Zoe St.
San Francisco, CA 94107

Dambrowski Nuttall Design Associates
621 E. 48th St.
Tempe, AZ 85281

Danielle Dimston
10 N. Main St.
Chester, CT 06412

Delany Design Group Inc.
68 E. Main St.
Providence, RI 02903

DeMartino/Schultz Inc.
233 Broadway
New York, NY 10007

Design Associates, Inc.
468 Park Ave. South
New York, NY 10016

Design Collective, Inc.
55 W. Long St.
Columbus, OH 43215

Design Investigation Group
338 Main St.
Racine, WI 53403

Design Works, Inc.
521 W. Ormsby Ave.
Louisville, Ky 40203

Din & Associates
415 N. Dearborn
Chicago, IL 60610

Eisenberg Inc.
4924 Cole Ave.
Dallas, TX 75205

Erwin Lefkowitz & Associates
4555 Henry Hudson Parkway
New York, NY 10471

Fataal & Collins
1119 Colorado Ave., Suite 104
Santa Monica, CA 90401

Mike Feldhouse Graphic Design
101 E. 9th Ave., Suite 136
Anchorage, AK 99501

Follis Design
2124 Venice Blvd.
Los Angeles, CA 90006

GGK New York
1515 Broadway
New York, NY 10036

Robert A. Gale Inc.
970 Park Ave.
New York, NY 10028

Gianninoto Associates Inc.
133 E. 54th St.
New York, NY 10022

Giarnella Design
43 Linwood St.
New Britain, CT 06052

Milton Glaser Inc.
207 E. 32nd St.
New York, NY 10016

Gorman Glassberg
156 5th Ave., Suite 224
New York, NY 10010

Goldsholl Associates
420 Frontage Road
Northfield, IL 60073

Gould & Associates
1100 Glendon Ave., #1500
Los Angeles, CA 90024

Graphic Design Works
4512 Kitridge Road
Dayton, OH 45424

The Graphic Suite
235 Shady Ave.
Pittsburgh, PA 15206

Malcolm Grear Designers, Inc.
391 Eddy St.
Providence, RI 02903

Tim Hartung
12919 Alcosta Blvd., #4
San Ramon, CA 94583

Herbst, Lazar, Rogers & Bell
415 N. State St.
Chicago, IL 60610

Hornall/Anderson Design Works
411 1st. Ave. South, #701
Seattle, WA 98104

Huerta Design Associates
3300 Temple St.
Los Angeles, CA 90026

Randall Hull Design Office
2241 Charleston Road, #200
Mountain View, CA 94043

IMS Graphic Services, U of U
205 Milton Bennion Hall, U of U
Salt Lake City, UT 84112

Image Dynamics Inc.
1101 N. Calvert St.
Baltimore, MD 21202

Dennis S. Juett
672 S. Lafayette Park Place, Suite 48
Los Angeles, CA 90057

J.C. Penney Co. Inc.
1301 Avenue of the Americas
New York, NY 10019

JTW Graphic Design
245 Greenwood
Glencoe, IL 60022

Kaneko, Metzgar, Ashcraft Design
228 Main St., #7
Venica, CA 90291

Kondziolka Takatsuki Design
4421 N. Harding
Chicago, IL 60618

Constance Kovar
300 Woodbury Road
Woodbury, NY 11797

Lam Design Associates
661 N. Broadway
White Plains, NY 10603

John K. Landis
438 W. Walnut St.
Kutztown, PA 19530

Landor Associates
Ferryboat Klamath
Pier 5
San Francisco, CA 94111

Lee & Young Communications Inc.
One Park Ave.
New York, NY 10016

Burson Marsteller
866 3rd Ave.
New York, NY 10022

Matrix International Inc.
3773 Cherry Creek Dr., #6901
Denver, CO 80209

McDermott Design
7777 Bonhomme, Suite 1504
St. Louis, MO 63105

Mielcarek Advertising
P.O. Box R
Staten Island, NY 10302

Paul D. Miller Enterprises
14 5th Ave.
New York, NY 10011

John Morning Design Inc.
866 United Nations Plaza
New York, NY 10017

Louis Nelson Associates, Inc.
80 University Place
New York, NY 10003

Carole Nervig/Graphic Design
2120 13th St.
Boulder, CO 80302

The Olson Group
610 Applegate Lane
Lake Zurich, IL 60047

Overlock Howe Consulting Group
4484 W. Pine Blvd.
St. Louis, MO 63108

Palam Design
933 Castille St.
Santa Barbara, CA 93101

Pushpin Lubalin Peckolick
67 Irving Place
New York, NY 10003

Regn/Califano
330 W. 42nd St.
New York, NY 10036

Rousso + Wagner Inc.
2045 Peachtree Road, NE #500
Atlanta, GA 30309

S&O Consultants
575 Sutter St.
San Francisco, CA 94102

SHR Communications
3001 N. 2nd St.
Phoenix, AZ 85012

Sandage Advertising & Marketing
215 College St.
Burlington, UT 05401

Shore Design
250 Columbus Ave., #203
San Francisco, CA 94133

Slesinger, Yaranoff & Associates
2214 N. Central Ave.
Phoenix, AZ 85004

Lauren Smith Design
2241 Charleston Road, #600
Mountain View, CA 94043

Standard Oil Co.
200 E. Randolph Dr.
Chicago, IL 60601

Studiographix
3501 N. MacArthur, Suite 411
Irving, TX 75062

Jef Sturm Graphic Design
1653 Merriman Road
Akron, OH 44313

Synthesis Concepts, Inc.
612 N. Michigan
Chicago, IL 60611

Robert W. Taylor Design
2260 Baseline Road, Suite 205
Boulder, CO 80302

Telesis
107 E. 25th St.
Baltimore, MD 21218

3D International
1900 West Loop South
Houston, TX 77027-3292

Visual Research & Design
360 Commonwealth Ave.
Boston, MA 02115

John Waters Associates
3 West 18th St.
New York, NY 10011

Wayfairer
2712 Glenwood, #15
Boulder, CO 80302

The Weller Institute for the
Cure of Design
2427 Park Oak Dr.
Los Angeles, CA 90068

Lance Wyman, Ltd.
118 W. 80th St.
New York, NY 10024

Richard Yeager Associates
39 E. Main St.
Moorestown, NJ 08057

Zahor Design Inc.
150 E. 35th St.
New York, NY 10016